Ethics and Reference Services

Topics in *The Reference Librarian* series:

- Ethics & Reference Services
- The New Technology & Reference Services
- Children & Young Adults Reference Services
- Cataloging & Reference Services
- Library Instruction & Reference Services
- Evaluation of Reference Services
- Conflicts in Reference Services
- Personnel in Reference Services
- The Reference Interview

Authors: See *MANUSCRIPT INQUIRIES*, copyright page.

Published:

Reference Services in the 1980s, Numbers 1/2
Reference Services Administration & Management, Number 3

Ethics and Reference Services

Edited by
Bill Katz and Ruth A. Fraley
School of Library & Information Science
State University of New York at Albany

The Reference Librarian
Number 4

The Haworth Press
New York

The Haworth Press, Inc., 28 East 22 Street, New York, NY 10010

Library of Congress Cataloging in Publication Data
Main entry under title:

Ethics and reference services.

(The Reference librarian ; no. 4)
Includes bibliographical references.
1. Reference services (Libraries)–Moral and ethical aspects.
I. Katz, William A., 1924- . II. Fraley, Ruth. III. Title. IV. Series.
Z711.E85 1982 174'.9092 82-11862
ISBN 0-86656-211-7
ISBN 0-86656-112-9 (pbk.)

Ethics and Reference Services

The Reference Librarian
Number 4

CONTENTS

Where Does It Hurt: Identifying the Real Concerns in the Ethics of Reference Service 1
Samuel Rothstein

Reference Ethics: A True Confession 13
Judith Farley

Value Laden Barriers to Information Dissemination 19
Dorothy Broderick

Reference Ethics—Do We Need Them? 25
Jack Clarke

The Ethics of Information Serving Homo Sapiens Vs. Homo Biblios 31
Emmett Davis

Toward the Development of an Informed Citizenry 45
Joan C. Durrance

User Fees: A Survey of Public and Academic Reference Librarians 55
Ron Blazek

Ethical Aspects of Medical Reference 75
M. Sandra Wood
Beverly L. Renford

Teaching the User: Ethical Considerations 89
John Lubans, Jr.

Ethics at the Reference Desk: Comfortable Theories and Tricky Practices 99
John C. Swan

The Unresolved Conflict 117
Melissa Watson

Some Ethical Problems of Reference Service 123
Patrick M. O'Brien

Ethics and the Reference Librarian 129
B. Strickland-Hodge

Ethical Considerations in the Question Negotiation Cycle 133
Richard Teller

Triage 143
Joan Meador
Craig Buthod

Regional Public Libraries and Reference Ethics 147
Debbie Schluckebier

Academic Libraries and Reference Ethics 151
Bea Flinner

Bibliographic Overview: The Ethics of Reference Services 157
Michael McCoy

The Reviewing of Reference Books 165
A. J. Walford

Forthcoming in *The Reference Librarian* 171

NOTE FROM THE PUBLISHER:

Our apologies to B. C. Vickery, A. J. Walford, Martha E. Williams, and Marda Woodbury, whose names were inadvertently omitted from the Editorial Board listing in issue number 3.

Ethics and Reference Services

WHERE DOES IT HURT? IDENTIFYING THE REAL CONCERNS IN THE ETHICS OF REFERENCE SERVICE

Samuel Rothstein

What is the right thing to do—for our clients, for our employers, for our government and society, for our colleagues and ourselves? In theory no subject would seem to be of more importance to reference librarians than the ethical considerations that underlie their activities. In fact the topic gets little attention.[1]

Bernard Vavrek, who is himself one of the few people to make a serious study of ethical issues, has deplored reference librarians' lack of interest in this subject.[2] His concern is commendable but the sad reality is that, considering the way in which the subject has usually been treated and presented, the apathy with which it has been received is understandable and perhaps even warranted.

The most common type of presentation has taken the form of a library association promulgating an official "code" or formal statement which presumes to set forth the principles and precepts by which the librarian is to be guided into righteous behavior. Some examples of such codes or statements are those issued by the American Library Association (1938 and 1975),[3] the Institute of Professional Librarians of Ontario (1975),[4] the Ohio Library Association (1976),[5] the California Library Association (1976),[6] the American Library Association (the 1979 revision of the 1975 version),[7] and the Library Association (1980).[8]

The failings of these documents are not difficult to detect. In a number of instances, notably that of the ALA Code of Ethics of 1938, the writing itself is so bad as to have prompted severe criticism. The "vague idealism,"[9] "fatuous adjurations"[10] and pompous platitudes[11] of such a statement are reason enough for ignoring it. Another problem is that the documents often mix up major points of principle with minor matters of etiquette.[12] Still another drawback, in this case more the fault

The author is a professor at the School of Librarianship, The University of British Columbia, Vancouver, B.C., Canada; and one of the leading authorities on the history and development of reference services.

of the library profession itself than of its codes of ethics, is that the codes are "toothless."[13] Librarians, in North America at least, are not yet so organized as to provide for investigation and punishment of malfeasance. Accordingly the precepts enunciated in the codes are regarded as pieties rather than rules of conduct.[14] Lastly, it should be noted that the codes tend to take a more unitary view of library practice than is actually the case. This is to say that the codes address themselves to librarians in general rather than specifically to public librarians, cataloguers, etc. In a profession as notoriously heterogeneous as librarianship, it thus becomes all too easy for librarians of a particular kind to dismiss the codes as having little direct relevance to their own situation.

As it happens, at least as of 1979, most of the above criticisms do *not* apply to reference librarianship. The revised version of "A Commitment to Information Services: Developmental Guidelines," which was originally issued by the Reference and Adult Services Division of the ALA in 1976[15] as simply its set of standards for information services, has added a section on "Ethics of Service."[16] This means that reference librarians have in effect a code of ethics of their very own.

The statement on "Ethics of Service" has much in its favor. The writing is refreshingly direct and succinct and for the most part its meaning is unequivocal. For example, reference librarians are enjoined to treat their "information contacts with users...with complete confidentiality" and are obliged to codify their rules and practices so that a "reference policy statement is to be made available to the user in written form."[17] It is to be noted that both of these "commandments," highly debatable though they are, are presented without qualification of any kind. The RASD statement on "Ethics of Service" is not afraid to speak its mind.

With so much to commend it, then, one would think that the RASD statement would have elicited considerable attention from reference librarians and perhaps even their applause. If this has in fact happened, I am wholly unaware of it. My own guess is that the statement has met with much the same sullen silence accorded to all its predecessor codes.

Assuming the accuracy of the above analysis, it seems to me that there can be only two tenable conclusions deriving from it: either reference librarians simply do not *care* about ethical issues or the whole matter has thus far not been presented to them in a way in which they would recognize the subject as being significant to them.

There being no hard facts to support either conclusion, I naturally prefer to take the most favorable view of myself and my fellow reference librarians. I assume therefore that reference workers *will* be ready to tackle their problems in ethics—i.e., in "doing things right"—if these problems can be accurately identified and properly analyzed.

Now, by far the best way of making such identification and analysis of ethical problems is simply to ask the reference librarians themselves—what conflicts, what difficulties, what tensions in their work lead them to question or to worry about whether they are doing the "right thing?" Unfortunately, we have had no such survey undertaken among reference librarians, but we can gain some idea of what such an investigation might yield by examining examples from allied fields. A very good case in point is the recent article by Eleanor Blum (herself a librarian) and Clifford Christians of "Ethical Problems in Book Publishing."[18] Blum and Christians adopted what they called "an inductive approach for [the] inquiry".[19] That is, instead of attempting to even define ethics, let alone enunciate precepts, they allowed "practitioners. . . to describe their own perceptions"[20] of the problems that had actually perturbed them. In almost all cases, they found out, the ethical problems of publishers center on conflict of legitimate interests. For example, concern about maintaining quality runs up against the need to show a profit; one's loyalty to the firm conflicts with one's obligation to the author, and so on. It should be added that the length, candor and emotional nature of the replies indicated clearly that the respondents *did* feel keenly about ethical issues if they were allowed the opportunity to say "where it really hurt."

It seems to me that the approach taken by Blum and Christians—to discuss the ethical problems of a group by focussing on the perplexities and anxieties actually felt by the practitioners—is also amenable and useful to a study on the ethical problems of reference librarianship. I propose, then, to do just that. Of course, not having seen or made a survey of reference practitioners' experience and opinions, I do not have any solid data at my disposal. No matter; I will make do as best I can without facts and, drawing simply on my own knowledge and imagination, attempt to describe what I think to be the actual situation. Acting then as both questioner and universal respondent, I now present my survey of the "real" ethical problems of reference librarians.

The most frequent and probably also the most important problems derive from the relationship between the reference librarian and the client. Because there is seldom any monetary advantage to be gained by the librarian whether his or her service be good or bad, the very considerable ethical conflicts and tensions implicit in the librarian-client "encounter" can easily be overlooked or misunderstood. Such problems, moreover, can be greatly compounded by virtue of the fact that the client seldom has the capacity or opportunity to judge the librarian's performance.

A good part of the difficulty in the librarians' dealings with inquirers arises, it seems to me, from the fact that the expectations placed upon the librarians seem so straightforward and simple—deceptively straightforward and simple. As a professional and therefore someone obligated to render service of an appropriate standard, the reference librarian must be, it is generally agreed, competent, assiduous, courteous and nondiscriminatory. Such aggreement, I suggest, is mostly the product of a rather superficial advocacy of what may look like the obvious "motherhood virtues." Examined more closely, each of the above desiderata may involve a sharp conflict between the librarian's self-interest and the interest of the client. Moreover, it is a conflict which the librarian may not necessarily or even usually be willing to resolve in favor of the client. Take, to begin with, the librarian's obligation for competence in the performance of his or her duties. This obligation implies not only the possession of the requisite initial qualifications (e.g., an M.L.S. with appropriate training in reference work) but also the requirement for keeping these qualifications up-to-date and up-to-scratch by a lifetime program of continuing education. This requirement for *maintaining* one's competence is, of course, no more than that which is demanded of professionals in almost every field. However—and here lies the ethical dilemma—unlike most other professionals, librarians are unlikely to receive much financial assistance or direct rewards for their efforts in continuing education, or, for that matter, to be subject to any penalty for *failing* to do so. Given also the fact that reference librarians are generally underpaid as it is and that their clients seldom recognize or complain of incompetence, should reference librarians realistically be expected to assume the burden of continuing education? The ethical problem here is substantial. It is also widely evaded, probably because, if seriously examined, it would really "hurt."

A comparable set of considerations apply to the other desiderata in the reference librarian-client relationship. It has been pointed out that reference librarians are frequently less than assiduous in the information service they render,[21] notably in respect of the degree of effort taken in the interview to find out exactly what the inquirer needs. Similarly, there is evidence to indicate that reference workers often discriminate among clients in the amount of service rendered. For example, questions from students and "contest" participants are likely to be treated quite differently than would the same questions asked by governmental officials or faculty members. Lastly, as librarians themselves have attested, courtesy and thoughtfulness are by no means the constant attributes of the reference worker. Crawford cites as particularly reprehensible the "casual disregard of confidentiality" in many reference departments and the "many put-downs" ranging from the "superior half-smile" to the "cold glare of indifference" by which librarians are apt to establish their superiority to their clients.[22]

The incidence of such failings among reference librarians in general is not known and is probably not even determinable with any statistical accuracy. Nor is it likely that individual librarians' performance in these respects is known either to themselves or to their supervisors. And yet knowledge is crucial in deciding whether an ethical problem is at issue here. Given the fallibility of mankind, *some* deficiencies in courtesy, effort or impartiality are inevitable in each of us. On the other hand, *consistent* failings in these respects would represent a kind of arrant insensitivity to the client's welfare that is tantamount to a dereliction in professional duty. And unfortunately the only way in which to answer that question of "guilt or innocence" is to have the individual librarians look within themselves and render conscientious and accurate judgment.

Clearly a substantial conflict of interest is implicit in such self-assessment. Quite apart from the normal human tendency to rationalize away one's failings and to take the most favorable view of oneself, reference librarians have some very good reasons to excuse or mitigate their blameworthiness. Others seldom appreciate in what extraordinarily difficult circumstances the librarian must operate within the "reference encounter." The reference librarians must serve anonymous clients whose needs and capabilities they cannot really know; they must be prepared to give instant answers to questions covering almost every conceivable subject; they must operate in full public view and under harassing requirements for speed. In most reference departments five minutes is considered a long time to allocate to one customer! Add in the facts that many of the questions asked may be repetitive to the point of numbing boredom and that the questioners themselves may be ignorant or rude, and is it any wonder that reference librarians may be tempted to take a self-exculpatory view of the imperfections in their relationships with clients? Here once again, then, the reference librarian's ethical problem will be "real" and substantial—and the dilemma will not be easily resolved.

Thus far in my analysis, I have dealt with the ethical problems of the librarian-client relationship solely in terms of the responsibilities devolving on the individual reference librarian. There is, however, another and very troublesome set of ethical problems in reference service which derive essentially from the policies set by the employing *library* rather than from the performance of the librarians themselves.

Perhaps the most publicized question of this sort relates to the *quality* of the information services rendered. The "unobtrusive testing" done by Childers and others has drawn attention to the fact that reference questions are often answered badly.[23] Allan Angoff has even suggested, albeit mostly facetiously, that libraries may be subject to malpractice suits if the erroneous or incomplete information which they supply leads to damaging consequences for the users thereof.[24] There seems to be no immediate likelihood of such suits but the mere possibility is enough to raise the significant issue of to what extent the library can and should "stand behind its wares."

And even if the library feels it can offer no guarantees, should it at least assume a commitment to quality in service? The Reference and Adult Services Division of the American Library Association evidently thinks the library should do something very like that. In the RASD's "A Commitment to Information Services: Developments Guidelines," it is specified that "a professional librarian/information specialist should be available to users during all hours the library is open."[25]

If the library is able but unwilling to meet that standard of quality, is it reprehensible? If it is unable, whether usually or in a given instance, to have a professional librarian of reference duty, is it morally bound to notify the public of that fact? If the library refuses to remedy or even give fair warning of its shortcomings in reference service, are its professional staff members and their library associations duty bound to take action against it? It will be readily seen that a whole hornets' nest of ethical problems opens up once one seriously examines the issue of quality control.

An even more explosive (pun intended, please note) issue in institutional responsibility was recently raised by Robert Hauptman's intriguing experimental study of libraries' attitude to the presumed *uses* of the information service they offered. Hauptman asked thirteen libraries for information on how to blow up a house; not one refused, on ethical grounds, to supply the information even though they were given reason to believe that the inquirer had a criminal purpose in mind.[26] D. J. Foskett once stated, in a memorable phrase, that the creed of a librarian vis-a-vis a client should be "no politics, no religion, no morals."[27] Apparently the libraries examined by Hauptman acted on those "hands-off" precepts to the point of being willing to aid and abet, so to speak, in the commission of a crime.*

Interestingly enough, the unanimity of viewpoint reported by Hauptman seems not to be unusual. In a rather similar vein, the library's obligation to respect the confidentiality of information about and for the client is one of the very few points to find a place in *all* the more recent codes of ethics. Such views probably derive from the present-day insistence on the paramount importance of freedom of information. However, as Hauptman points out,[28] in their anxiety to avoid imputations of censorship, discrimination and bias, libraries may well be abjuring other responsibilities to society. There is a real conflict of values here, no less strong for being generally unrecognized.

The issues of neutrality and privacy are also interesting in that they are examples of what may be said to be "gray areas" in reference ethics.

Doubt breeds dispute, and in such gray areas there are likely to be many instances of where conflicts of principle and interest arise *as between* the librarian and the library. An example may illustrate the point. How much reference service is the client entitled to? The conscientious librarian may well feel that any thing less than an effort at full satisfaction is "short-changing" the client. Such a view may run counter to a library's policy of limiting service in the interest of economy.

It is probably a safe generalization to say that within the last decade, public libraries have been willing to go much further in the provision of *legal* reference service than ever before. There is no evidence to suggest that similar courage or initiative has been applied to other categories of "sticky questions." The traditional reluctance of libraries (as distinguished from their staff) to deal with matters of controversy is still evident in the way in which they tend to treat inquiries regarding the merits of specific encyclopedias, dictionaries and other reference books. Here on their very own ground of expertise, so to speak, reference

---

*Robert Pierson has called attention to the fact that reference librarians quite frequently "aid and abet" in the commission of *academic* "crimes" such as plagiarism and cribbing. Cf. his "Is Moby Dick the Whale or the Captain?" *RQ* 7:21-24 (Fall, 1967).

librarians are usually not permitted to offer their personal knowledge or opinions and can only direct inquirers to such information as may be available from published sources, such as reviews. The libraries' caution is presumably occasioned by fear of prompting criticism or legal action by publishers. But such pragmatic considerations can run counter to the conscience of reference librarians themselves, who may see themselves as ready and able to do a far better job of information service than the needless timidity of their employing institutions allows them to offer.

Some of these conflicts between reference librarian and library *might* be obviated or alleviated if the libraries were required, as the RASD "Developmental Guidelines" demand,[29] to prepare and make public a written statement of reference service policy. The conscientious reference worker, who finds a given program of reference service to be substandard, would then presumably know that fact in advance and not go to work for such an employer. One may even visualize library associations protesting against and imposing sanctions upon such an offending library, much as the Library Association (of the U.K.) urges its members to blacklist libraries held to be in violation of standards of proper practice. Moreover, the poor old clients, now almost always completely ignorant of their rights in respect of reference service, would then at least know what they are entitled to expect, and might even press for a higher standard of service.

It is worth noting, however, that the result of requiring libraries to make a public statement on their reference policy might well yield the opposite outcome to that visualized above. My own guess is that such publication would prompt many libraries to play it even safer than they do now. They would simply employ opaque or evasive language to cover themselves against troublesome demands or criticisms. In a sense their commitment to a really good reference service might be weakened rather than strengthened.

Some Personal Conclusions

The fact is that there is probably no way in which the conflicts of interest or priorities as between librarian and library can be wholly reconciled. The same is probably true for *all* the examples of conflict which I have given in this paper. Moreover, I am convinced that it is a very good thing that the problems described here are *not* all that easily to be remedied.

I may well be deluding myself into taking an unreasonable optimistic view of an intractable situation, but it seems to me that it is the very existence of numerous and substantial ethical problems that attests to librarians' claim to professionalism. It is just because we recognize ourselves as having obligations and duties that may well outweigh our self-interest; it is because we espouse principles and standards that may well bring us into conflict with our employing institutions and even governments (as in the matter of confidentiality cases); it is because we may place duties upon ourselves (e.g., for continuing education) which our employers do not even see as necessary—it is largely because of issues such as these that we may distinguish our responsibilities as professionals from those of law-abiding persons of any calling.

I note with relish, moreover, that reference librarianship provides more and keener instances of such ethical concern than do most other types of library work. Reference work provides the practitioner with a clearly visible (if usually anonymous) client and a readily available and reasonably accurate judgment of success or failure in one's efforts on behalf of that client. By contrast, the technical services librarians cannot usually obtain nearly so immediate or sharp a sense of the consequences of their actions on the people they serve.

Accepting, then, that reference librarians not only *do* but *should* have ethical problems, how do I suggest that they deal with them? My recipe consists of three steps. The first is to dispense with attempts at preparing or following codes of ethics. The consistent lack of attention given to such codes, not only in librarianship but in other fields,[30] indicates that they are of little use.* Almost inevitably they are apt to be pompous and orotund in wording and vague in meaning. More important, they are likely to be pointless and boring. People at any time do not wish to be harangued by precepts (I seem to recall that even the Ten Commandments did not go down very well with its intended audience)—all the more so if those precepts are unenforceable and, because of their generality, of doubtful relevance to any one group.

Nevertheless—point two—ethical issues *can* be confronted. Indeed they *must* be if we reference librarians are to regard ouselves as anything more than technicians. The first requirements in such confrontation is to identify the issues that really matter. I have suggested that the way to

---

*For a contrary conclusion regarding a field closely related to librarianship (information science), see the recent and interesting article by B. J. Kostrewski and Charles Oppenheim, "Ethics in Information Science," *Journal of Information Science,* 1: 282-283, (January, 1980). A code of ethics, say Kostrewski and Oppenheim, would be useful in committing the professional association "to a certain stance in the case of a dispute between an information scientist and his employer." (p. 283)

do so is look within ourselves and see what troubles us—where it hurts. Many such troubles—our anxieties about the right thing to do, our conflicts of interest—will be easily apparent from such self-analysis. (Whether to charge fees for reference service is a pertinent and at present frequent case in point.) Other problems we, like all other humans, may well have tried to repress or ignore. (The ethical obligation to maintain our professional proficiency is an example of such generally unacknowledged problems.)

My last point is that, having (perhaps at some pain) identified our ethical problems, we must reconcile ourselves to not solving them. As distinguished from minor questions of deportment, which are amenable to prescription in "codes of practice,"[31] major questions of principle, priority and conscience can only be discussed and debated, not decided. But such "inconclusive" debate and discussion are still well worth undertaking. At worst, it will indicate to ourselves and to the general public that librarianship is not the bland, colorless, routinized activity that it is too often reputed to be.* At best, we reference librarians will individually receive useful guidance on the very biggest and most significant of the problems that beset us.

And it all begins by finding out "where it hurts."

REFERENCES

1. Robert Hauptman notes that Daniel Gothie's extensive *Selected Bibliography of Applied Ethics in the Professions 1950-1970* does not include a single citation in the field of library science. Cf. Robert Hauptman, "Ethical Commitment and the Professions," *Catholic Library World* 51:197 (December, 1979).

2. Bernard Vavrek, "Ethics for Reference Librarians," *RQ* 12:56 (Fall, 1972). Much the same complaint is made by Shirley Fitzgibbons, "Ethics," *ALA Yearbook 1977.* (Chicago: American Library Association, 1977), p. 116.

3. American Library Association. Code of Ethics Committee, "Code of Ethics for Librarians . . . Adopted . . . December, 1938," *A.L.A. Bulletin* 33:128-30 (February, 1939); American Library Association. Special Committee on Code of Ethics," Statement on Professional Ethics . . . 1975," reprinted in *ALA Yearbook 1976* (Chicago: American Library Association, 1976), p. 155.

4. Institute of Professional Librarians of Ontario, "I.P.L.O. Code of Ethics," *I.P.L.O. Quarterly* 17:88-91 (July-October, 1975).

5. Ohio Library Association, "Library Code of Ethics, of the Ohio Library Association," *Ohio Library Association Bulletin* 46:7-9 (January, 1976).

---

*Cf. John Sharp's biting criticism of librarianship in this regard. He avers (mistakenly, in my opinion) that "the professional ethic is relevant only to situations in which there is potential for good or evil. Librarianship is sterile in that respect." ("For Good or Evil, Librarianship is Sterile," *Library Association Record,* 83:192. April, 1981.)

6. California Library Association, "Draft Statement of Professional Responsibility for Librarians," reprinted in *Recurring Library Issues: A Reader,* ed. by Caroline M. Coughlin (Metuchen, N.J.: Scarecrow Press, 1979), p. 413-419.

7. American Library Association. Professional Ethics Committee, "Draft: Statement on Professional Ethics, [1979]," *American Libraries* 10:666 (December, 1979).

8. Library Association, "Draft Code of Professional Ethics: a Discussion Document October, 1980," *Library Association Record* 82 (October, 1980). Unpaged insert.

9. Martha Boaz, "Code of Ethics, Professional," in *Encyclopedia of Library and Information Science,* (New York: Marcel Dekker, 1971), v. 5 p. 246.

10. Samuel Rothstein, "In Search of Ourselves," *Library Journal* 93:156 (January 15, 1968).

11. John G. Fetros, "The Search for a Code of Ethics," *American Libraries* 2:744 (July, 1971). Cf. also Eric Moon, "Ethical Bones," *Library Journal* 93:131 (January 15, 1968) and Helen Crawford, "In Search of an Ethic of Medical Librarianship," *Bulletin of the Medical Library Association* 66:331 (July, 1978).

12. E.g. the A.L.A. Code (1938), point I.8; the Ohio Library Association code, points V.2,3,4; the I.P.L.O Code point 7.

13. Crawford, "In Search of an Ethic of Medical Librarianship," p. 331.

14. The Library Association and the California Library Association codes are interesting exceptions to this statement in that they *do* make provision (not yet implemented, I believe) for the associations to review complaints of misconduct against members and to impose sanctions if need be.

15. American Library Association. Reference and Adult Services Division. Standards Committee. "A Commitment to Information Services," *Library Journal* 101:973-74 (April 15, 1976).

16. *RQ* 18:275-78 (Spring, 1979).

17. *Ibid,* p. 277

18. Eleanor Blum and Clifford Christians, "Ethical Problems in Book Publishing," *Library Quarterly,* 51:155-69 (April, 1981).

19. *Ibid.*, p. 156

20. *Ibid.*

21. Donald Davinson, *Reference Service* (London: Clive Bingley, 1980), p. 93-96. Davinson bases his conclusions largely on the research by G. Carlson, *Search Strategy by Reference Librarians: Final Report on the Organization of Large Files, Part 3* (Sherman Oaks, Calif.: Advanced Systems Division Hughes Dynamics Inc, 1964) [NSF Contract C 280]

Cf. also Thomas Childers, "The Test of Reference," *Library Journal* 105:926 (April 15, 1980); David E. House, "Reference Efficiency or Reference Deficiency," *Library Association Record* 76:222-23 (November, 1974); William A. Donovan, "The Reference Librarian and the Whole Truth," *RQ* 8:196-99 (Spring, 1969)

22. Crawford, "In Search of an Ethic of Medical Librarianship," p. 334-35.

23. Thomas Childers, "Managing the Quality of Reference/Information Service," *Library Quarterly* 42:215 (April, 1972).

24. Allan Angoff, "Library Malpractice Suit: Could It Happen to You?", *American Libraries* 7:489 (September, 1976).

25. "A Commitment to Information Services: Developmental Guidelines," p. 277.

26. Robert Hauptman, "Professionalism or Culpability? An Experiment in Ethics," *Wilson Library Bulletin* 50:626-27 (April, 1976).

27. D.J. Foskett, *The Creed of a Librarian—No Politics, No Religion, No Morals* (Library Association. Reference, Special and Information Section. North Western Group. Occasional Papers No. 3 [London: Library Association, 19662]).

28. Hauptman, "Professionalism or Culpability . . . ," p. 627.

29. "A Commitment to Information Services: Developmental Guidelines," p. 277.

30. Boaz, "Code of Ethics, Professional," p. 246.

31. Cf. Institute of Professional Librarians of Ontario "Recommendations re Professional Conduct: Some Do's and Don'ts for I.P.L. Members" [*I.P.L.O.*] *Information Bulletin* No. 4 (March, 1962).

ADDITIONAL REFERENCES

Anderson, John F., "Ethics: the Creaking Code," *Library Journal* 91:5333-35 (November 1, 1966).

Dalton, Jack., "Ethics" in *ALA Yearbook 1976* (Chicago: American Library Association, 1976), p. 155-56.

Donovan, William, "Seemingly Unjustified Complaints Repay a Second Look," *RQ* 8:265-67 (Summer, 1969).

Gibson, Barbara, "Professional Ethics for Librarians," *British Columbia Library Quarterly* 27:10-13 (April, 1964)

Grogan, Denis, *Practical Reference Work*. London: Clive Bingley, 1979, p. 16-17, 110-112.

Katz, William A., *Introduction to Reference Work: Volume II, Reference Services and Reference Processes*. 3d. ed. New York: McGraw-Hill, 1978.

Roberts, Anne, "Prescriptive, Descriptive or Proscriptive? Implications of the Developmental Guidelines, A Commitment to Information Services," *RQ* 17:223-25 (Spring, 1978).

Vavrek, Bernard, "Implications of the New Information Service Guidelines," *American Libraries* 6:295-96 (May, 1975).

REFERENCE ETHICS: A TRUE CONFESSION

Judith Farley

As a child enrolled in the Philadelphia Catholic school system, I dreaded one weekly examination above all others. I never passed. Every Friday afternoon, Sister would say, "Now, children, it is time to prepare for confession tomorrow. Use the next ten minutes to examine your consciences." Admittedly, this examination was silent, self-administered, and self-marked, but I failed it every time. My sins of omission and commission flashed neonlike in my bowed head. I would never remember them all. Should I write them down to make sure I could recite them in the confessional? But what if I lost the list? Then everyone, not just God and Father Cunningham, would know what a sinner I was.

I dredge up my shameful past now because writing this article has entailed the same sort of examination of conscience. Would I, the editor asked, discuss the practical aspects of ethics and reference service, drawing upon my personal experience? And in such a way that other librarians could find guidance for their ethical dilemmas? Flattered that anyone should think I had the answers, I agreed. And then came to a full stop. What, I wondered, were the questions?

Legal and medical questions seem the most fertile fields for a discussion of ethics. But the Main Reading Room of the Library of Congress is a general reading room. To my colleagues in the Law Library, the Science Reading Room, and the National Library of Medicine, therefore, go these weighty matters. Instead, I find that my ethical dilemmas are more usually generated by the type of reader than by the question.

Open to anyone of college age or older for 77 hours a week, the Main Reading Room serves an average of 9,738 readers a week.[1] The reference staff of 14 answers approximately 3,566 questions a week. If you divide the latter figure by the former, it seems obvious that we can't

Ms. Farley is Reference Librarian, The Library of Congress, Washington, D.C. 20540.

spend a lot of time with each reader. At the Central Desk one day, a woman asked me for assistance in finding pictures of the Berlin Wall and the Iron Curtain. I found several sources of photographs of the wall, but suggested to her that the Iron Curtain was a metaphor used by Winston Churchill in 1946 to describe the Soviet sphere of influence. No, she corrected me, the Iron Curtain was a physical entity of which the Berlin Wall was an extension. They were built of different materials, the wall from brick and concrete, and the curtain, of course, from iron, but both were real and she needed pictures of both. By this time, five other patrons were waiting. In desperation, I suggested she check the catalog under the heading "Communist countries—description and travel," and she seemed content.

Later, in a discussion of difficult reference questions, I recounted this incident to colleagues at ALA. There was sympathetic laughter, but one friend protested that I had failed in my duty to educate the reader. Rather than entering into her misapprehension, my friend said, I should have insisted that she face reality. In retrospect, I believe I served that woman poorly, but at the time I chose to move on to the waiting readers.

That incident calls to mind several others involving patrons who are disturbed. Some months ago *The Washington Post* ran a story featuring several LC patrons with notable idiosyncrasies. Reading it, several friends remarked that I must have some funny stories to tell and asked for more details. In this instance I declined, because the *Post* account had angered me, making me feel protective toward those readers. It is sometimes tempting, however, to describe an amusing encounter with a reader, and I do fall from grace occasionally. How much confidentiality can a reader expect from a reference librarian?

If a scholar engaged in writing a book asks me to say nothing about the subject and progress of his research, it is easy to oblige. If a reader wants to speak to me privately because she needs help in locating shelters for abused wives, I ask no questions. But I'm afraid that the blanket prescription contained in the RASD guidelines: "Information contacts with users, whether reference or directional, are to be treated with complete confidentiality,"[2] sets an impossibly high standard for reference librarians. I do not advocate its revision, since one should strive for perfection, but I do ask for recognition that it is the ideal.

While these standards promulgate the obligation to provide accurate information, they are silent on the ethics of the information-gathering process. One morning a businessman needed extensive information about a local business. We found balance sheets, stock records, annual reports, but he also wanted specific sales data. After trying several sources in vain, I suggested he call the company's sales manager. Because his own firm was in direct competition with this company, he was unwilling to telegraph his interest. He asked me to request the information officially on behalf of the Library, or, better still, for a Congressman's office. When I refused because such a gambit was unethical, he was surprised. "I thought," he said cuttingly as he departed, "that librarians were creative." Creative or not I am daily in contact with a variety of readers whose library expertise and expectations of service differ widely. I find myself guilty of disparate treatment of patrons; the ethical issue arises because of the subjective judgment exercised in each case. For example, following the dictates of social conscience and consciousness, I usually offer more help to a poor-looking reader than to a prosperous one; to the very old and the very confused rather than to the self-assured.

It seems reasonable at first thought to offer more guidance to a first-time user than to a regular patron, until one realizes that often the steady parton is a neophyte in gathering information outside his/her narrow field of scholarship. Library school students are in a class by themselves. Since they must learn by doing, I usually encourage them to read the preface and introductions of reference tools themselves rather than explaining how to use them in detail. The rule I try to follow, and the only advice I can offer, is the aphorism, "To each according to his need."

A related issue concerns helping people find information in support of positions to which you are philosophically or morally opposed. One afternoon, for example, a young man told me that his workplace was being organized by a union. His employer wanted him to compile a list of strategies and tactics other companies had used to circumvent the union. I happen to be a strong union supporter, believing that all workers have the right to organize.

I also believe in the Library Bill of Rights, which states in part:

> Libraries should provide materials and information presenting all points of view on current and historical issues. Materials should not be proscribed or removed because of partisan or doctrinal disapproval.[3]

In this instance, however, it struck me that the Bill of Rights remains silent on a librarian's obligation to lead people to the materials the library holds. Reluctantly recognizing that this argument was hair-splitting in the classic Jesuitical tradition, I showed the young man how to find the information he wanted. Occasions for such private conflict can arise with distressing frequency; the only answer I've found is to grit your teeth and do your public duty. But I did not wish that reader luck on his project.

Deciding whether or not to accept a gift from a reader seems an easier question to resolve. I do not, of course, mean payment for services rendered; that must be illegal as well as unethical. But at times a reader is so grateful for assistance that it would be offensive or undiplomatic to refuse a sincere gesture. Three examples here: a woman presented me with a copy of her newly published first novel. She was very excited and wanted to show her appreciation for some help I had given her in the course of her historical research. On another occasion an official from an embassy whom I had taken on a tour of the Library gave me a packet of postcards showing his native city; he hoped that some time I could tour his country's national library. Finally, one morning an elderly man brought me some cookies his wife had made. The day before, I had spent considerable time teaching him how to use the Library's computerized data bases. His wife wanted to thank me for providing her husband "the most fun he's had in a library in years." How could I refuse?

I want to emphasize that the solutions found to the questions above are personal rather than institutional. My division's manual for reference librarians contains no section on ethics, although the Library's regulation 2023 on personal conduct and activities governs all staff members. Reference librarians in other institutions may have specific policies prescribed by their employer. The Library Bill of Rights, the ALA Statement on Professional Ethics,[4] and the RASD standards provide helpful guidelines, but these statements cannot be inclusive or specific enough to cover every awkward situation which may arise. Ultimately, I believe that reference ethics are a mixture of instinct, tact, discretion, and common sense. Or, as my eighth grade teacher, Sister Marietta, was fond of reminding us, "Let your conscience be your guide."

NOTES

1. Based upon an hourly count of the reading room. Of course, many readers are counted more than once.

2. American Library Association. Reference and Adult Services Division. Standards Committee, "A Commitment to Information Services: Developmental Guidelines" (section 6.3). *RQ*, v. 18, Spring 1979: 275-78.

3. As amended January 23, 1980. In *ALA Handbook of Organization 1980/1981*, p. 196.

4. The 1975 statement and the draft revision appear in *American Libraries*, v. 10, Dec. 1979: 666.

VALUE LADEN BARRIERS TO INFORMATION DISSEMINATION

Dorothy Broderick

As a non-reference specialist, teaching a course in Public Libraries, all I wanted for my class was a sample of a Reference Service Policy. Perhaps they exist in the private files of many libraries; they appear not to exist at all in public sources.

The case studies books on reference stress the nature of the collection or the difficulty in locating particular types of information. Occasionally, a case study will deal with some aspect of a service policy; e.g., should a library provide contest answers, but generally, writings on reference service limit themselves to building the collection and providing answers. This approach strikes me as ignoring the fundamental question: namely, who shall be served?

When a library fails to develop a service policy, the result is that the individual librarian is given free reign to impose his or her own biases. Since many, if not most, of these biases are unconscious, a service policy serves in effect as a consciousness raising tool.

Until recently, it seemed safe to say that at the very least the white, middle class, educated segment of a population would find itself receiving adequate reference service in a library. That assumption is now in question as demonstrated by the following examples.

In *The Library Promotion Handbook,* Marion Edsall relates the following experience:

> Just recently I had occasion to seek some information about an unusual geological formation off the coast of Belize, in Central America. I went the usual route of consulting the card catalog and and the indices with which I am most familiar but found nothing. Time was running short, so I "bothered" the reference librarian on duty with a request for assistance to hasten the search. And bother

The author is editor of *Voice of Youth Advocates* and Professor at the Graduate School of Library Services, University of Alabama, University, AL 35486.

> it obviously was, although she was not particularly busy; she waved airily toward a shelf, and said, "Well, I don't know...did you try that index over there?" She promptly turned around to something else on her desk. It was a classic example of the waving-arm-over-there syndrome.[1]

Edsall is one of the lucky people. She is a trustee of the library system to which the library belongs and when she recounted the incident to one of the library administrators, a few days later she received a book providing the information she needed.

Andy Hansen, Executive Secretary of ALA's Reference and Adult Services Division, tried for service over the telephone. All he wanted to know was whether the U.S. government had a consulate in Glasgow, Scotland. After two tries, he took himself to the library and found the answer.[2]

If service to the white, middle class is getting worse, one can only hypothesize about the service being given to the less favored of society. Reference librarians are ordinary people who happen to have (or are supposed to have) some special skills generally lacking in the public they are expected to serve. This means that their personal value systems and biases interfere more with the reference service given than do inadequate skills.

While it is possible to subdivide almost indefinitely the following statement, in general, I submit that reference librarians make value judgments about the information being requested and the person doing the requesting.

For example: some years back a man clearly of Mexican American descent walked into the reference room of a large southwest library on a Sunday afternoon. He was dressed in muddy overalls. He asked the librarian for information concerning worm farming (at that time a very new concept). She treated him and his request with ridicule; it was all a big joke to her.

It ceased being a joke the following Wednesday night when the Mexican American President of the City Council recounted his experience and asked if that type of service was what they were paying good tax money for. The entire library was indicted because of one librarian's behavior. Personnel in that library now wear name tags so that the sinning individual can be identified.

The literature of psychology is filled with similar experiences, mostly with commercial stores. Two people of same sex, same age, same race, are sent into a store. One is well dressed, the other is scruffy. Guess who is offered prompt service by the store personnel? In another experiment, race is made the distinguishing feature, and whites receive service before blacks. As Billy Pilgrim is fond of saying, "So it goes."

At the library school in Rutgers, a reference professor sent students out in pairs to ask the exact same reference question of the same librarian to see if the personal qualities of the patron influenced the service provided. One such couple consisted of an elderly library trustee, taking the course to better understand the library he was making policy for; his teammate was a hippy type young lady. They both told the librarian, "I want some information on demonstrations." The hippy type young lady was given information on the then current demonstrations in Berkeley and other campuses. The elderly trustee was given information on how to obtain a demonstration permit!

The bias concerning the age, racial/ethnic background, and type of information being sought is not limited to public libraries. In university libraries, the least well served patron is the undergraduate. Status of the patron is clearly a determining factor in service provided. It is a bias that all reference librarians must admit to themselves before they can begin to overcome it.

Age bias becomes even more important when the patron is a child or adolescent. There is a general assumption on the part of librarians (both those hired to serve children and those in other departments) that children should limit their interests to subjects that are adequately covered in the children's room. When I lived out in the country in Nova Scotia, my small store had a sign that read, "If we don't have it, you don't need it." I often feel it more properly belonged in the libraries I used. And I am sure children, even if they are unable to articulate the concept, share my feeling.

Many of the children who use public libraries today (approximately 50% of the youth population) are very knowledgeable about computers, stereo components, and other technological devices that remain mysteries to older folk. Yet it is a continual hassle for these elementary kids to obtain information on the level they need it because someone has determined that some books are for adults and some for children. The fact that many adults need the books written for children and many children are quite capable of mastering the material supposedly for adults only, escapes many librarians. Moreover, to categorize the material rather than to assess the borrower's level of competency and need is to demonstrate an appalling lack of understanding concerning the learning process. I realize that many librarians pride themselves on their ignorance of institutional design and other educational processes, but such ignorance is a defect, not an attribute.

There is a further age bias here, that against the material itself. When developing interlibrary loan codes, many libraries make it a policy to not borrow children's materials. That the request may come from a person working on a doctoral dissertation or a scholarly history of the literature seems not to occur to many reference librarians. In saying that, I do not mean to imply that I would approve of a policy that made exceptions based on the possible use a patron was going to make of the materials being requested.

In fact, of all the biases demonstrated by all librarians (reference, circulation, adult, young adult, children's), the one that bothers me most is that pertaining to judgments made about potential use. Let an adolescent walk up to the reference desk and ask for information on abortion, contraception, homosexuality, and one can almost see the librarian mentally saying, "I'm not sure I want this kid to have information on *that*." On the other hand, let the same adolescent say, "I'm interested in colleges with a strong pre-medical program," and the librarian is off the chair and providing more information than the young adult needs or wants.

Value judgments about the use of material place us in the same category as the most virulent of community censors. They, too, are sure that if the potential for misuse of information exists, it will be misused. That is a very poor view of the human race, one I do not share. I am convinced that most people, given access to all points of view, will choose for themselves, that which is least destructive personally and for society. I worry far more about decisions based on ignorance than those based on information, however disagreeable that information may be to me personally.

A less politically negative aspect of making judgments about the use of material concerns telephone reference questions that are deemed "school work" by the answering librarian. Just why it is somehow more appropriate to help a student unearth "school work" answers in person than over the telephone remains one of life's great mysteries to me. It appears to be in some way connected with an idea about "doing the work" for the student in question. The idea that there is something inherently educationally worthy about the search process itself as opposed to the use made of the material once it has been located again demonstrates a lack of understanding as to what education is and ought to be. Learning to evaluate the material is far more important than learning to locate it, yet often, so much of a student's time is taken up with the search process that little time remains to put it to good intellectual use.

Finally, a few words about bias against information formats. Except for school media specialists and special librarians, librarians are still wed to the idea that valid information exists in books or it doesn't exist at all. The lack of audiovisuals in most public and college libraries is appalling. The fact that few patrons are ever given the opportunity to view a 16mm film as the answer to their information needs is a disgrace. The same can be said for information on filmstrips, cassettes, and phonodiscs. We must now add such "modern" tools as computer data bases and videodiscs.

Much of the responsibility for the perpetuation of these biases rests with the library schools. Too much emphasis is put on where to find an answer and not enough on the relationship between the librarian as a person and the patron as an equal. It is not possible for a good library school teacher (or even a good library school) to change the attitudes and values of students by dicta. It is possible to establish the environment in which those students capable of change do change. Many students are quite willing to examine their personal prejudices and work toward eradicating them once they have consciously become aware of them. Making students aware of their biases has a high priority in my view of what education means, or ought to mean.

During a recent election in the Tuscaloosa area, there were signs all over the roadside reading, "Santini is the answer." Very good, I thought, but what, dear Santini, is the question? Reference librarians ought to be searching their souls to see if they, like the politician, are focusing too much on the answer when the question remains unknown.

NOTES

1. Edsall, Marian S. *Library Promotion Handbook*. Oryx Press, 1980. pp. 19-20.
2. Hansen, Andrew S. "From the Desk of the RASD Executive Secretary." *RASD Update*, Vol.1, Number 3 (September/October 1980), pp. 11-12.

REFERENCE ETHICS—DO WE NEED THEM?

Jack Clarke

Reference librarians have long cherished the idea of providing their patrons with a direct, personal, and impartial service that permits no restrictions on the amount and kinds of information they will supply. "The only tenable, impregnable theory of reference work," James I. Wyer wrote in his famous textbook, "is that which frankly recognizes the library's obligation to give this unlimited service."[1] Wyer speaks of the "ethics of self help" by which he means training patrons to a moderate independence "and little more." In her fine text Margaret Hutchins discusses briefly the "Ethics of Publishing Reference Questions." But Louis Shores' immensely popular textbook during the 1950s and into the 60s has little to say on ethical aspects of the reference function.[2]

To complement and to explain their noble objective most well-organized reference departments have devised both written and unwritten staff procedures and standards of ethical conduct. Ethics is usually defined there as the principles of conduct governing an individual or a group. These prescriptive rules usually form a part of each library's staff manual and may also be expressed in its public service code. Few practitioners realize, however, that the self-imposed restraints so often set by local policies on confidentiality and other aspects of reference, can substantially limit the extent and quality of the service to be performed.

No two librarians will handle a sensitive question precisely the same way since practice varies so widely by size and type of library. This inconsistence may stem partly from our failure to develop over the years "a system of theory to elucidate, justify, and control practice."[3] Or perhaps our library school training may have neglected the ideological aspects of reference service. It is uncertain whether the pragmatic basic

---

The author is a professor at the Library School, University of Wisconsin, Madison, WI 53706. He thanks David Henige, African Studies Bibliographer at the University of Wisconsin-Madison, for reading several drafts of this paper.

reference courses taught in so many library schools deal with the issue of ethics more thoroughly than in the past.

In order to cope successfully with ethical problems at the reference desk we must first develop a sound theory of professional practice. The ideal reference librarian is poised and helpful without appearing inquisitive; she is tactful but specific and persistent in identifying the information that is needed. She recognizes her patrons' desire for privacy and respects it. She knows that there are secretive researchers on every campus who hide their ideas and view reference librarians with suspicion. There are also people who come to her regarding health problems, legal difficulties, or an impending divorce. Is it ethical for the librarian of either sex to blush or behave nervously during the reference interview and the subsequent search and then to discuss the reference interview with her colleagues?

A careful examination of *Library Literature* under the general heading ETHICS reveals a continuing concern with professional credos, public relations, and polite and tactful behavior. Both articles and brief notes as well as letters to the editor are based on long experience and are therefore pragmatic in nature. "Loyalty to fellow workers and superiors," a practically oriented writer noted "even blind loyalty, is of first importance."[4] Only a small part of these common sense canons by "well-bred" librarians applies to reference services however. "Public confidence in our discretion and approachability," one writer added, "is more important than a reputation for always being right."[5]

Association efforts to set ethical guidelines for reference services have accelerated in recent years. There is a distinct increase in the number and quality of both individual and committee reports on this protean topic.[6] In 1979, after long deliberations, the Reference and Adult Services Division formulated standards of service that include these main points: Accuracy, confidentiality, equity or impartiality, and absence of personal gain. In their view information/reference service must always be impartial and nonjudgmental. The concept of good service is impossible unless these points are scrupulously observed. Yet "one discerns apparent disinterest [sic] among reference librarians," a shrewd observer of librarianship notes, "This is rather curious when it would appear that individual principles of conduct affect reference librarianship more than any other library activity."[8]

Despite appreciable differences in meaning the terms "unprofessional" and "unethical" have often been used interchangeably. Thus, a reference librarian who answers a complex question about the national debt but fails to identify the source or sources is guilty of unprofessional conduct or at least, sloppy work but no more. A librarian who refuses to attend a convention or participate in committee work is also unprofessional. So too might we regard as unprofessional a librarian who refers a sensitive question to another desk in the library without consulting the patron's wishes. She assumes that our patrons will not object to a breach of privacy provided the answer is quick and accurate.

We move over the line to unethical conduct when a librarian regales colleagues in the break room with the news of some unsavory ancestors recently discovered by a well known local genealogist. A reference librarian who reacts coldly to a question about busing (remarking that she disapproves of it) may be a competent searcher in this regard but she is guilty of questionable ethical conduct. Self discipline and sensitivity are clearly required here. Providing extra time and effort for a favorite patron, who occasionally brings a box of chocolates, is also unethical. Conversely, a librarian who zealously guards the anonymity of circulation records but allows unauthorized personnel to inspect files of socially sensitive reference questions is being both unprofessional and unethical. So too is a subject or area studies bibliographer who refuses to serve undergraduates or the bibliographically unsophisticated. In short many reference librarians are more interested, at least overtly, in supplying requested information quickly than in maintaining a high standard of ethical practice.

One of our allied professions, archival administration, has also recently focused its careful attention on ethical considerations but from a very different standpoint. By definition, archivists select, preserve and afford access to both public and private material of lasting value. However, archivists often have to contend with donors' restrictions that can limit access to unique manuscript collections for years, or reserve them for a single, donor designated, researcher. This is particularly true of oral history programs. On one midwestern campus retiring administrators are routinely interviewed about the efficiency and philosophical orientation of their former peers and supervisors. Naturally, these information files must be closed to the general public for years in order to protect outspoken openness and tactless remarks.

It is not unusual for an archival patron to complain bitterly at the curator's desk that there is damaging information about unsavory aspects of his business or personal life in someone else's papers. Citing his right to privacy, he demands that this collection be closed to the public during his lifetime. In a few instances patrons have asked that unflattering remarks be expunged from the official records. In the new profesion of data archivists similar ethical questions have arisen concerning, for example, who owns the evidence and statistical results for government sponsored research. It also appears that archivists working with machine-readable data must develop special procedures to protect rights to personal privacy.[9] If this is not done, archivists may find themselves in the precarious situation "of assuring confidentiality while at the same time maximizing access to and use of these materials."[10] To forestall such embarrassing contre-temps the archival profession has adopted a code of ethics "based on sound archival principles [in which they] promote institutional and professional observance of these ethical and archival standards."[11]

Do we need a code of reference ethics which would be flexible enough to provide guidance to most reference librarians yet at the same time specific enough to lend support to a librarian who has a specific ethical dilemma? This is a hard question—one that deserves more time and thought from harried practitioners than it usually gets. To compile such a code that will serve equally public, special, and school libraries is both labor-intensive and time consuming. It must deal with the privacy of individuals as well as the right of groups to collective privacy, be they ethnic, racial, or religious minorities. Moreover, there is no solid evidence that codified rules and practices appreciably improve the efficiency or accuracy of our public services. A code must always take into account the desired level of performance as well as the institutional framework for their work assignments. Clearly, further study is needed.

Many practicing reference librarians regard written codes as "bureaucratic nonsense." No model code can be devised, it has been argued, that is applicable to all libraries and accepted by most librarians, "human nature being the sensitive and paradoxical stuff it is."[12] Some librarians are reported to fear that "the potential result [of developing] a code might resemble a taxonomy of platitudes that would suit everyone and no one simultaneously."[13] Others see a code as an essential element in professionalism that should be made available in written form to new staff members and of course distributed to all our patrons. In this discerning view the library profession must formulate positions on its major ethical questions, and put them into practice in consistent ways.[14]

This writer has no quick and facile answers for these difficult questions. The issue is raised here and now to emphasize that every so often each reference librarian ought to ponder the problem caused by a breach of confidentiality just to prove to herself that it still exists. We would argue that individual librarians ought not to discuss a specific incident with colleagues, but it does seem useful for the staff to discuss issues concretely in general and anonymous terms. Preparation for this type of high-level professional discussion would very well begin with role playing exercises in a library school reference class.

It also appears from discussions with practitioners that the more friendly and personal the relations between reference librarians and patrons the less need for a formal code which can slow down and complicate the reference process. Tact and good sense alone can provide a better understanding of goals between these two disparate groups. If a code is deemed necessary, however, it ought to be interpreted liberally in order to achieve this good understanding with a minimum of dissention. Accurate, impartial, and non-judgmental responses to their questions, based on a sound search strategy, appears to be the "great expectation" that most of our patrons want from us.

REFERENCES

1. James I. Wyer. *Reference Work: A Textbook for Students of Library Work and Librarians.* Chicago: American Library Association, 1930. p. 9.

2. Wyer *op. cit.* p. 7. Margaret Hutchins. *Introduction to Reference Work.* Chicago: American Library Association, 1944; p. 194-195. Louis Shores. *Basic Reference Sources: An Introduction to Materials and Methodologies.* Chicago: American Library Association, 1954.

3. Pierce Butler, "Survey of the Reference Field" in *The Reference Function of the Library, Papers Presented before the Library Institute at the University of Chicago June 29-July 10, 1942.* Chicago: University of Chicago Press, 1942.

4. Agnes Brindley. "Library Ethics" *Wilson Library Bulletin* 15:417. January, 1941.

5. Louis F. Ranlett. "Libraries Have a Word for It: Ethics" *Library Journal* 64:740. October 1, 1939.

6. Reference and Adult Services Division. Divisional/Standard Committee Meeting *LC Information Bulletin* August 25, 1978. See also on this topic, California Library Association. California Society of Librarians. Draft Statement of Professional Responsibility. *RQ* 15:241-244 particularly on the last page, Principle 4. Spring, 1976.

7. "A Commitment to Information Services: Developmental Guidelines" *RQ* 18:275-278. Spring, 1979. See Part 6.0 Ethics of Service p. 277.

8. Bernard Vavrek. "Ethics for Reference Librarians" *RQ* 12:56-58. Fall, 1972.

9. Margaret Hedstrom. *Privacy, Computers, and Research Access to Confidential Information.* Presented at the Spring Meeting of the Midwest Archives Conference at Chicago. May 2, 1980. p. 15.

10. See "Chapter 5: Confidentiality and Privacy" in *Archivists and Machine-Readable Records.* Edited by Caroline Geda and others. Proceedings of the Conference on Archival Management of Machine-Readable Records. February 7—10, 1979, Ann Arbor, Michigan. p. 191.

11. *A Code of Ethics for Archivists.* n.p., n.d.

12. Mary A. Kernan. "Professional Responsibility" *Wilson Library Bulletin* 31:523-24. p. 524. March, 1957.

13. Vavrek. "Ethics for Reference Librarians" p 58.

14. Eric Moon. "Ethical Bones" *Library Journal* 93:231. January 15, 1968.

THE ETHICS OF INFORMATION SERVING HOMO SAPIENS VS. HOMO BIBLIOS

Emmett Davis

Librarians must temporarily set aside ethical codes and re-engage ethics as a process. Our profession should be undergoing remarkable development as it attempts to reconcile new awareness of undeserved population, the impact of new technologies, the growth of information conglomerates, and resource limitations. We as a service community have not sufficiently analyzed the foundations of our actions.

When rules are easily, widely, indeed unconsciously followed, they are studied by sociologists and internalized by children, strangers, and other "uncivilized barbarians." These are unwritten codes and cover such essentials as wearing clothes to work and church. Assuming there are principles behind our behavior, sociologists inductively attempt to articulate them.

The rest of us rarely note these living codes, and instead focus on rewriting such standards as the ALA Library Bill of Rights. In these instances, we record in a semi-contractual manner principles and generalizations which apply to our behavior. With these statements we warn employers, promise potential users, and prod colleagues to extend or limit service. We decode these declarations through precedents, normal English reading, and local compromises.

These ethical codes must advocate possible behavior, a point of contention among those opposing that behavior. The goal being sought must be reachable even in these times of increasingly scarce resources. The charge that a code is impossible to implement should be fatal to a code's consideration. This charge, however, is also misused and incorrectly raised when behavioral changes are resisted for social and cultural reasons. While it is possible, although difficult, to grant full library rights to children, disabled people, and cultural minorities, it is impossible to serve the dead. The charge of impossibility was recently raised in a review of Emmett and Caterine Davis's book, *Mainstreaming Library Service for Disabled People* (Scarecrow, 1980).

The author is with the Hennepin County Library, Edina, MN 55435, and author of *Mainstreaming Library Services for Disabled People*.

> They demand that information service "be found in the library by all who need it," without realizing that this requires a library that currently does not exist, since no library presently tries to service all who need it. Such a library would be required to serve the illiterate, the blind, the bedridden and the astronauts in space.[1]

The reviewer tried that old logic test, *reductio ad absurdum* and failed. The charge against the ethical stand taken by my sister and myself is serious. If it had been true, it should have sent us back home to rework our proposal. The strength of our stance is that today libraries do serve a wide variety of needs. I know Minnesota libraries best and we DO serve illiterate and blind patrons with audio materials and oral responses in person and over the telephone, bedridden people with materials mailed from the library, and if an astronaut had called I am sure Minnesota librarians would have read the information back over the telephone, "Yes, California does have a hangy-down part. It is Baja California between the Pacific Ocean and Mexico."

The ethical standard we offered in *Mainstreaming* was:

1. All humans are, during at least part of their lives, open to the social aspects of a library.
2. All humans learn and change and should be able to draw on the library for support.
3. All humans have a right in the library to learn in the manner best suited to them, individually and socially.
4. Library staff, the library as an institution, and the community must be fully open to serve all. There should be no silent refusals by omission.[2]

All this is not only possible, it is actual. All we are asking is that present resources and changes that normally come along in the life of a library be more efficiently handled so as to maximize service.

Extensions of service, research on service in new situations or with new techniques, and the acquisition of new types of materials and technologies when proposed in an environment of limited resources are, however, more than questions of technical efficiency. Our expertise as librarians might allow us to efficiently use resources, but whether to apply these resources for a specific purpose is a political decision based on values.

The values underlying *Mainstreaming* and many ALA standards arise from a centuries old humanism. This humanism has been studied as a general cultural movement, with its roots being traced back beyond the industrial revolution. What has not been studied as well are the traditions that oppose this humanism, especially in libraries. What has been the cultural basis for denying extensions of service when that denial has gone beyond mere lethargy or inadequate resources? If articulated would these values enrich Western Civilization or the major religions of homo sapiens? What universal values underlie the political decisions of:

a) a librarian acting in *loco parentis* to children selecting "adult" material,
b) only English language service being offered in a community where other languages flourish, and
c) removing material from circulation because it is objected to by members of the community?

We must try to abstract from this behavior in a positive and analytical manner principles which could then be discussed.

Among a wide variety of librarians, there is a common belief in the library's power to change and influence people. Librarians, who despair of the values and behavior of their community governed by radio and television, patterns of violence and social disintegration, and dropping educational standards, consider library activities in their citadels to be a *beau geste.* Yet these same people, with other librarians, unshakably assume that an inquiring free mind if it absorbs *The Lottery* in film form, Judy Blume's *Forever,* or nonsexist/nonracist material will powerfully be influenced for good or evil. How light patterns on a page or a screen can influence a person's behavior or that of a community are as poorly understood as they are assumed to be operative.

While many of our values have not been analyzed, the need for a commonly understood set or sets of values is continually intensifying. Since the time when the Carnegie libraries were first designed, our society has "discovered" disabled people able to be served by libraries, new information technologies with linear and nonlinear information applications, and industrial conglomerates that can re-organize information dissemination into profit making patterns. Members of our society other than librarians are organizing access to information within these situations. Federal law 504 requires access to services for disabled people. That is, library standards have been legislated outside the walls of our institutions. We were behind society when it came to understanding the needs of disabled people. Other members of our society control the new technologies and the mass dissemination of information. Either we have our affairs controlled by legislatures or we are only another market. We have been bypassed.

Concerned over whether or not we have our library in order, we believed it to be a storehouse of treasures. We may awake to find that it is an outhouse and there are great things doing up in the manor. We librarians have not commonly been either the patrons or the companions of scientists and innovators of new technologies, members of the Disability Rights Movement who almost as an afterthought in their struggle demanded their public library rights, or publishers as they either sold out or resisted the commercial "unprofessionalization" of their industry. While capable of berating as uncultured and illiterate those who do not cherish printed material as we do, too many of us can only leave the room when baud rates, boolean logic, pixilation, digitalization, and other information related terms are used. Many of us are illiterates in the universe of information. True we know where the 921s are shelved. But have we insured that all the information material not shelved in our library is also accessible to the community we serve?

The responsibility for creating access to materials located outside the walls of our local library is not restricted to one geographic place (THE NATIONAL LEVEL) or to one caste of librarians (THE POLICY MAKERS or THE ADMINISTRATORS). We all are responsible, each reference librarian, each children's services librarian, each cataloger. We are as responsible as if this were a direct democracy.

If there would be one segment of our profession that bears more responsibility than others, it would be reference librarians. They are the cutting edge of our field, out where the needs of people are washed up on the shores of our information land. They see which needs reach safe harbors and which are stranded on archaic subject headings and insufficient subject analysis, on a poverty of viewpoints because only large press material has been acquired, or on incompatable learning media where, for example, a person who needs audio formats finds only printed material.

The reference librarian is also best able to define a library to a community. When an individual wishes to read a book that is not sought after by ten million others, it is the reference librarian taking a reserve who can say, "Oh, it is no trouble for me, but God help the poor soul who has to process this reserve." It is these public service staff who can alienate those whose interests are not wrapped in cellophane.

It is the reference librarians who see the need for material in audiovisual media, languages other than English, a variety of reading levels, and a diversity of cultural environments. Reference librarians are the first to learn the defects of their collections. With their knowledge, it is the duty of us all to not place the burden for being different on potential users. We are a grand people when we proclaim intellectual freedom and yet tailor our services to clones of ourselves.

We must learn to serve homo sapiens and not just the subspecies homo biblios. Homo biblios love books. Even when they do not often read them, they swear by them. Homo sapiens, on the other hand, are multisensory beings. Some homo sapiens prefer to learn from and prosper within a strong linear, intellectual interpretation of the world. Other homo sapiens learn best in a variety of modes (audio, tactile, and combinations). Not all homo sapiens, either in the United States as a whole or in individual states such as Minnesota, read printed English well.[3]

Homo biblios, or any other subspecies of homo sapiens, when organized can efficiently perform such tasks as strip mining an entire county. When dealing with complex systems, however, like terrestrial ecology, non-oppressive social systems for producing and distributing wealth, and reality and non-reality, the strength of the species is manifest when projects consist of teams of homo sapiens of various learning modalities (visual, audio, tactile), cultures (patriarchical/matriarchical, hierarchical/egalitarian, Anglo/Hispanic/Amerindian/*et cetera,* straight/gay, urban/rural/suburban, disabled/temporarily-abled-bodied) and personalities (dominant-submissive/team-oriented). In designing the institutions called libraries, we have underemphasized both the contribution each homo sapien, indeed each element of creation, is offering the universe and the support that records of knowledge can provide each homo sapien during portions of their lives to maximize those contributions.

That libraries serve homo biblios better than other subspecies is evident in that the information, both questions and answers, that all can use is recorded in libraries mostly in print form. When fees for service are necessary to defray the expenses of the library, why is it that the normal use of books is exempt, while any use of films and data bases are subject to a tax? Why is one mode of learning privileged? Even when we do not actively tax, deny service, or otherwise harass the general homo sapien population, we fail them. We may know our archives well, but have we learned enough about how people learn both individually (as teachers and educational psychologists know) as well as socially? What models or hypotheses are we operating under when we work with or design library service for humans? How do we modify those models, through research or day-to-day public service?

While codes of ethics are often used as tools of political control, other ethical aspects of our work, such as individual and group self-reflection, can be an even more potent tool to assist us in understanding who we are. This search for self-knowledge would have pleased Socrates, although many reformers and conservers would rather get down to the practical uses of ethics. Ethics is not merely right-or-wrong on two tablets. It is a process which always has as its goal the utilitarian concern of shaping behavior. Although that concern has been channelled into legislatures such as ALA where control over others has been sought, a more effective use is a socratic, non-legislative use where ethics as a process works on oneself and one's community the way a Greek gadfly's questions once did.

The reason ethics as a process can work so strongly on us and indeed what gives libraries their power is that like members of most social and many bisexual species, we operate with only a "half-a-deck." We barely understand reality, while at the same time are capable of learning more. Learning never ends.

For some, though, a sense of satiety comes from assuming the adequacy of what they already are given, even if it is similar to a geocentric view of the universe. Cultural satiety is comfortable because what we know is a whole and adding to it or changing a portion upsets or resets everything else. Information, what a cultural being knows, is relational, rather than just an aggregate of isolated facts. We can learn more, can be aware of how little we know, and still survive.

The perception of the limitation of what we know is two edged. It applies to the communities where we live and serve, giving our role as librarians as great if not a more practical significance than that of other civil servants. But it also applies to ourselves and to what we know and, more terribly, what we need to know as librarians. Again while we know where the 921s are shelved, do we know how people learn? How do we ourselves know or perceive?

What librarians offer is perception based service. Given infant socialization, puberty, peer instruction on the social aspects of the world, and library school instruction on bibliographic records, we practice our profession. We interpret similar bourgeois ethical standards in a variety of ways, depending on the four above givens. The wide, indeed the increasingly wider, variety of practices has bothered some, leading to the attempt to codify our ethical standards in such a way that specific types of behavior are approved (applause) or condemned (hiss).

These ethical codes should sting and burn when they are not followed. Too often we neutralize a code by doing what that reviewer above had done to *Mainstreaming*, declaring it to be visionary, unreal. We detach it from the details of our library and our community. We declare it to be a non-political document.

Now if an ethical code succumbs to such labelling, then it deserves to be so treated. But if there are people in the community and the library who determine that, whether visionary or not, a code is practical and worthwhile, then that code becomes a social issue and comes alive. What that code has become is not the reflection of a mind, but a reflection of how a portion of us behave. You or I can outline alternative ways of living, but only living those ways can make ideas effective. There is a notion in the popular mass media that the Classical Greek gods actually existed but were powerful only when they were worshipped. When they were forgotten, they became ineffectual, visionary and unreal. So codes are baubles if they do not stir local hearts. If they penetrate into the needs of people, these same codes can link people leading to rising expectations and channelling of actions.

Ethics to be effective must be close to being successful, to being lived, for there is a social dimension to ethics. What we do, not what we intend to do, is the most important aspect of our work. How can we democratically and non-directively serve a community with a non-democratic institution led by a director? How can we serve a heterogeneous society when we select for homogeneity among ourselves? Library personnel and users shape the design of service. We determine what we do. If the "we" is the community, then information institutions will occasionally be asked to perform new tasks. Although some libraries measure success with budget and circulation increases, communities have more varied measures. The production and distribution of status and wealth is one concern. The ability to survive as a gene pool in a viable natural environment for millenia may be another concern.

Although the most visible component, ethical codes are a small part of the process of ethics. The greatest share of ethical work is daily carried out by our co-workers as individual staff members. They are the people who fine tune procedures to fit values they have internalized. They are the ones who are bothered by exceptions and weather pressures to change. While pretty statements of intellectual freedom may hang on library walls, it is the daily actions of staff and community that constitute intellectual freedom and other ethical patterns. Curiosity is either a daily affliction, or it is dead. Questioning, looking at data, sharing hypotheses, recording elements of the learning process, decoding records (print and audiovisual) produced by others; all these are habits and built into the rhythms of a culture's and a society's normal existence, or they are alien.

Even the most practical among us do not operate with the resources available, but only with resources *as they are perceived*. To control our perceptions would be like inventing the lever, we could move the world more than we could dream. Socrates and his students, Siddharta, Mozart, Christ, and many others did so much in lands with a lower GNP than ours. We are our most significant limitation, both because we limit ourselves more than anything else and because we are capable of changing and learning.

Yet in spite of this, ethical codes overlook our perceptual distinctions. All men are created equal (except women, People of Color, children, seniors, emotionally ill persons, . . .). Thou shalt not kill (unless thou art soldiers, police, national liberators, . . .). The library provides information (except pornography, third world/small/alternative press material without three reviews, non-print, non-English language material, . . .). To all (except disabled people, non-English language users, illiterate people, people with unusual information needs, . . .) for free (except for fees for films, art prints, data base use,...). Codes are naive. They do not take into account either what divides and differentiates us, or what unites and makes us the same. We librarians are all clothed (even shoe-wearing), bourgeois, acculturated, adult, Anglo homo sapiens. We are so, so very much alike. Codes ignore this similarity. We librarians are so different from the world we serve. We differ with large segments of human kind culturally and economically. And again codes ignore this difference.

Yet most codes, as blind as they are, urge us to create libraries that serve more. Because libraries directly serve so few, so very few, are we to take a stance that the *Mainstreaming* reviewer took and point to this urging on the part of codes as a defect? Is the defect in the codes that goads us to serve all, or in our information institutions that serve so few?

How can we insure that libraries as an information disseminating process will provide information to each one of us as we need it?

Usually the question is worded so that the topic seems to be only whether or not certain kinds of information ought to be provided. But since information sought in libraries is sought by specific people requesting specific information, refusal to provide access to a type of information is denial of service to this or that category of people.

There are two opposing schools of thought on this topic. One school surfaces in the writings of librarians ranging from Mevil Dewey (the "question of excluding the pernicious . . . is the great problem of the modern library, and its solution must depend largely on the State."[4]) to Robert Hauptman (who found that the reference librarians who helped him build a bomb in the mid-1970s did not consider their actions "within an ethical context. . . . That they were generally overly helpful is intolerable."[5]). The other approach appears in defenders of intellectual freedom, including D. J. Foskett (*The Creed of a Librarian—No Politics, No Religion, No Morals*)[6] and in questioners of our current practices such as Leonard Wertheimer ("Pornography in the Public Library, Are Librarians Ignoring Its Role?")[7] and Michael Pope (*Sex and the Undecided Librarian).*[8] The problem (as Foskett phrases it) is that,

> we must have a philosophy, an attitude of mind according to which one action will be right and another wrong. If we have this, we can make our decisions with confidence; for although we may not have the right to censor, to tell people what they shall not read, we do have the right of our office, the right to decide what shall be in our libraries and what shall not.[9]

Dewey was confident that there was "pernicious" material to be excluded. Hauptman believed that staff are valuing beings with ethical commitments to withhold information on topics ranging from abortion to bombs as opposed to "a rather dubious professional commitment (viz., dispensing information)."[10] Foskett held that librarians with strong personal convictions are to be preferred—all librarians should assume a professional stance of being both "enthusiastically involved with the programme of a particular reader, and still remain outside the narrow limits of his special interest. . ."[11] Wertheimer and others merely raise problems with the present practice of free access to information without taking "into account existing laws, political factors or human nature."[12] As Michael Pope wrote, "Librarians give strong support to the concept of intellectual freedom and open access to the information but do not necessarily implement these concepts in their libraries."[13]

As a response we can echo Thomas Jefferson and others, stating that information/records are powerful. Not because of a "dubious professional commitment" but because of a living belief in the healing power of information, we withhold as little information as possible. Only privacy and other rights limit dissemination. If you consider such actions as bomb making or abortion to be incorrect, then use social control mechanisms that exist outside the library. While we are valuing beings, to limit the flow of information is an improper act, a nonhealing, nongrowing act. The beliefs of librarians posit informed right action on the part of information users only in the long run. To balance this requirement to not limit information, it is our duty to provide more information, to backup our trust in the healing power of free information by promoting discussion and insuring that the widest range of information and ideas possible are available. The error is not that information on abortion or bomb making is available, but that that information alone is available without material on human life and human inflicted death having been previously accessible.

To act professionally for the first time by limiting knowledge, by censoring, is to react violently, without balance and both destroys the basis of future growth and is a poor, self-serving substitute for what should have been a long history of action and thought to rectify the imperfections of our world. If the life of a fetus is holy, then what measure can be placed on the structural violence imbedded in our world of ecology destruction, hunger, war, and oppression? If you feel that you are a valuing being, rather than steel yourself for a future time when you will deny information, begin now with thought, discussion, emotion, and action in concert with others to change the world, leaving open the possibility that you yourself will change. Just as peace is not an absence of war, so intellectual freedom is not merely an absence of restrictions. Intellectual freedom is a vibrant contending of ideas.

Are we in a period alive with ideas? When people want to expand, to develop, do they go the the library? There are aliens in town; will they and we learn to communicate? There are irreplaceable resources being churned into local subdivisions; will we learn to live as a self-regulating species? There is intentional oppression of citizens; will we learn to identify and overcome handicapist, printist, ageist, anglocentric, racist, sizist, sexist behavior? While we share curiosity and a belief in meaning and communication with other homo sapiens, the unique contribution of our profession is our capacity to doubt, thoroughly and broadly, information and records. It is a gift to be able to question the actions and beliefs of our service beyond both our immediate perceptions and that of our culture.

What is the purpose of our service, especially in our multicultural society? Often the answer is visualized as a librarian at a reference desk assisting a patron with a sequel of the patron absorbed in a book. But the purpose I am seeking is at another level. The purpose of medical service is to provide individuals with health care, often to restore health and alleviate pain. Beyond individual purposes, however, there are institutional objectives. In the armed forces, medical services increase the efficiency of a war machine, enabling injured soldiers to return to health and the battle to either destroy or be destroyed. So what is our purpose? Do we ultimately serve individuals or institutions, society, and culture?

Perhaps some of us are willing to announce that libraries should serve either individuals or groups, but can we as a service community document that we do in fact serve one or the other? We have not adequately studied the impact libraries have had on either society or individuals. We may have anecdotal material or statistics on this or that characteristic, but where are the studies analyzing either the cultural or the social impact of libraries?

We cannot even describe the role of literacy, of the ability to decode printed records, in society or an individual's life in precise ways.[14] Our most precious treasure, print material, is a mystery to us. Here I mean mystery in a pejorative sense. It is one thing to be in awe of the beauty of a system in operation, such as a gothic cathedral after you have studied architecture, but it is quite another to fumble in the dark, to refuse to analyze and question, to be pompous while standing on hazy assumptions and the kudos of pleased patrons. We are unable to even explain the functioning of print, let alone our tinny-tiny role in the print structure.

For sure you can get friends of the library, or a public poll, or circuit speakers to place libraries between Motherhood and Apple Pie. But on what basis are they judging us? Is it after years of hard, systematic, precise, questioning analysis, or is it founded on prejudice and anecdotes? We value information and records, but do they help us to be more wise and more human because of the way we have organized them in libraries?

Recall Socrates's warning about the origins of our libraries—the Middle Eastern invention of phonetic writing—

> For this invention will produce forgetfulness in the minds of those who learn to use it, because they will not practice their memory. Their trust in writing, produced by external characters which are no part of themselves, will discourage the use of their own memory within them. You have invented an elixir not of memory, but of reminding; and you offer your pupils the appearance of wisdom, not true wisdom, for they will read many things without instruction and will therefore seem to know many things, when they are for the most part ignorant and hard to get along with, since they are not wise, but only appear wise. . . . And every word, when once it is written, is bandied about, alike among those who understand and those who have no interest in it, and it knows not to whom to speak or not to speak; when ill-treated or unjustly reviled it always needs its father to help it; for it has no power to protect or help itself.[15]

When tired, I doubt.

I doubt whether any individual or group can contribute enough to correct information systems (including libraries) as they malfunction today.

I doubt whether libraries contribute much to the development of our civilization, our species, as it attempts to mature before it destroys itself and its world.

When rested, I question.

I question why the American Library Association's most prominent recent achievement is as a real estate developer in a state that has yet to ratify ERA.

I question why we organize library institutions on hierarchical models derived from military organizations.

I question why we fail so miserably to serve those who differ from ourselves.

I question why so few of us attempt to understand the basis of libraries, literacy, information, and learning.

FOOTNOTES

1. Milton S. Byam, "Book Review of *Mainstreaming Library Service for Disabled People*," *Science Books and Films*, volume 16, number 4 (March/April 1981).

2. Emmett A. Davis and Catherine M. Davis, *Mainstreaming Library Service for Disabled People* (Metuchen, New Jersey: Scarecrow, 1980), p. 52.

3. "The United States Census figures for 1970 show that there were 54½ million adults, sixteen years and over, who had not completed high school. Of these persons, 23½ million finished only eight years of school; two and a half million had less than five years of school.

"The Texas Adult Performance Level Study, a national research survey released in 1975, revealed that one out of five adults, age eighteen to sixty-four, is functionally illiterate . . . one-half of the population is merely functional and not proficient; a widespread discrepancy exists between what is required of adults in American society and what they are actually able to achieve." University of Minnesota. Literacy Committee, *Literacy in Minnesota: People and Programs* (1978), pp. 1-2. I recommend this work as a tool for structuring your exploration of local literacy and Adult Basic Education programs.

4. Melvil Dewey, "The Relation of the State to the Public Library," *American Library Philosophy: An Anthology*. Selected by Barbara McCrimmon. (Hamden: Shoe String Press, 1975), p. 2.

5. Robert Hauptman, "Professionalism or Culpability?" *Wilson Library Bulletin*, volume 50, number 8 (April 1976), pp. 626-627.

6. D. J. Foskett, *The Creed of a Librarian—No Politics, No Religion, No Morals* (London: Library Association, 1962).

7. Leonard Wertheimer, "Pornography in the Public Library, Are Librarians Ignoring Its Role?" *Canadian Library Journal* (February 1980), pp. 21-26.

8. Michael Pope, *Sex and the Undecided Librarian* (Metuchen, New Jersey: Scarecrow, 1974).

9. Foskett, p. 6.

10. Robert Hauptman, "Ethical Commitment and the Professions," *Catholic Library World*, volume 51, number 5 (December 1979), p. 198.

11. Foskett, p. 11.

12. Wertheimer, p. 25.

13. Pope, p. 184. "Many of the categories in this study which are rejected by large numbers of librarians are works in science, medicine, history, sociology and art. Because of the sexual association of these books, librarians are willing to say that these books are inappropriate for their libraries." Pope, p. 184.

14. Among the literature on literacy is the thought-provoking work of Harvey J. Graff, *The Literacy Myth: Literacy and Social Structure in the Nineteenth-Century City* (New York: Academic Press, 1979). "Literacy was both act and symbol; it was neither neutral, unambiguous. nor radically advantageous or liberating. Its value, in fact, depended heavily on other factors, from ascribed social characteristics such as ethnicity, sex, or race, to the institutional, social, economic, and cultural contexts in which it was manifest. The role of literacy in the life of individual and society is contradictory and complex." Graff, p. 19.

15. Plato, "Phaedrus" in Harold North Fowler, translator, *Plato With an English Translation* (Cambridge, Massachusetts: Harvard University Press, 1953), I, pp. 563-567.

TOWARD THE DEVELOPMENT OF AN INFORMED CITIZENRY

Joan C. Durrance

> In a political system grounded in an informed citizenry, librarians are members of a profession explicitly committed to intellectual freedom and the freedom of access to information. We have a special obligation to ensure the free flow of information and ideas to present and future generations.
>
> *ALA Statement on Professional Ethics, 1981*

One of the major goals of public librarianship has been the development of an informed citizenry. However, the responsibilities which librarians must assume to ensure "the free flow of information" to citizens have not been clearly articulated. One principal reason has been that the ethical tenets which underlie these obligations have not been adequately discussed within the context of the librarian's relationship to specific client groups. The ethical relationships of most professions are examined within the client-professional interface. The findings of recent research on the information needs of specific groups suggest that the ethical considerations can best be understood within the framework of a specific client-librarian relationship. If we select as the client group the "informed citizenry" libraries seek to develop and limit that group even more to the citizen who attempts to participate in the community decision making process, we have the basis for a discussion of the responsibilities of reference librarians toward a group with specific needs. Ethical questions which arise from the act of providing access to public policy information for a specific user group provide the grist for discussion. The questions discussed in this article include not only those which grow out of ALA's Code of Ethics, but also the ethical considerations associated with our neutrality position and our curious quest for anonymity and its effect on the accountability

---

Ms. Durrance is Coordinator of Continuing Education, School of Library Science, University of Michigan, Ann Arbor, MI 48109.

of the profession. Discussion will be within the framework of the public policy information needs of citizens who desire to be adequately informed about community problems.

Up to this time, there have been few models of public policy information service based on citizen need. However, experimental models are beginning to emerge. For example, the Fairfax (Va.) County Library provides a computer-based information service linked to the State Legislative Data Base in Richmond, Va., making rapidly changing state legislative information available to local citizens. The Denver Public Library's Regional Energy/Environment Center was developed to help people "through the maze and confusion which confronts them when they need energy/environment information;" and Dallas Public Library's experiment in public policy information service, Public Interest Information Network (PIIN) was targeted "to meet the information needs of government agencies and citizen advocacy groups faced with local public policy questions" (Clayton, p. 23; Durrance, 1979, p. 234).

Citizen Activism - Background

This researcher has been involved in studies of citizen group activity in Toledo, Ohio; Madison, Wi.; Ann Arbor, Mi.; and Dallas, Tx. (Durrance, 1979; Durrance, 1980). The purpose of these studies has been to analyze citizen group activities and the information behavior which results from these activities; its aim has been to provide librarians with methods which can be used to understand local citizen group activities. The focus of the research has included analysis of the conditions which precipitate citizen group activity, the specific activities developed in response to community problems or issues, information needs resulting from citizen group activities, and the problems associated with gaining access to the information needed to become "informed citizens" on the topic of concern. A number of questions have arisen in the course of this research regarding the ethical responsibilities of librarians. To develop a framework for the discussion of these questions, the role which these groups play in a democratic society and the problems they encounter as they seek information will be presented prior to a discussion of the ethics of information service delivery.

The Role of the Citizen Group in a Community

The number of citizens which form into groups to solve community problems or influence public policy decisions has increased markedly in the past decade. Indeed, the recent activities of conservative groups has focussed the attention of the popular press on these groups and their activities just as the news media spotlighted those of the antiwar activists of a decade ago. However, in every community there are groups of individuals of various political persuasions, as well as groups with no perceptible political leanings, whose primary aim is to work toward solving community problems or to influence decisions which are made on issues which affect the public. These citizen groups include nationally affiliated organizations and a host of special interest groups developed to solve narrowly defined problems.

Research has shown that the rate at which citizens in general participate in solving community problems and influencing community decisions (even to the extent of contacting a local official to express an opinion) is overall quite low. In the early 70s (latest available figures) only six percent of citizens actually engaged in even the simplest activities (Verba & Nie: 1972, p. 354). However, even though their actual numbers in comparison to the overall population are small, citizens from all segments of society join with others into citizen groups for the purpose of solving community problems or discussing and/or acting on issues which affect the community. In fact, citizen group activity is an important boost to a community's poorer citizens. Verba and Nie postulate that if the rates of membership of disadvantaged populations in citizen groups were to increase, the political participation disparity between them and middle class citizens would be reduced (Verba & Nie: 1972, p. 207).

Citizen groups act as positive influences in their communities in other ways. A Gallup Poll conducted in 1978 and billed as "the state of the cities report" showed strong approval by citizens of the activities of citizen groups, particularly neighborhood groups (McBride, 1978). The findings of the report show that citizens in general approve of the activities of organized citizens and across the country indicate a willingness to become involved at the local level either by endorsing the actions of these groups or through assisting the groups in their community work. Because these groups represent pluralistic perspectives, they are microcosms of their communities.

Problems Citizens Encounter Obtaining Information

The problems encountered by citizen group leaders in gaining access to needed information raise questions about the responsibility of librarians to increase access. ALA's introductory statement on professional ethics affirms that librarians are committed to "freedom of access of information" but the code itself is silent regarding the obligations of the librarian to increase access. Research in several cities shows that citizen groups encounter common barriers in gaining access to information, yet often citizen groups do not think in information terms. Some do not even consider that they are seeking information. They are solving problems, but in order to be effective, they need information. The relative access (or lack of) which a group has to information is a factor which affects the group's style of action. "Information is power" is more than just a cliche. In the early stages of solving a problem or influencing an issue, citizen group leaders may be unfamiliar with the terminology used by bureaucrats or with the specifics of agency procedures. They also have problems determining which agencies to contact or what specific government programs or regulations mean. Valuable time is often lost as citizens attempt to find pertinent information. The nature of the decision making process involving bureaucratic or legislative structures which are only sporadically tapped by citizens results in a citizen knowledge gap; this means that citizen groups are handicapped when they try to influence policy makers. The increased knowledge-information gap which occurs at the beginning of a project puts the group at an even greater disadvantage *vis-a-vis* the decision maker. If this gap is not decreased in some way, such as through access to appropriate information, increased confrontational activity by the citizen group is likely to occur or the group may prefer to operate its campaign through the media. Indeed, some groups never obtain access to adequate information.

The barriers to gaining access to information which have been identified by citizen group leaders seem to be associated most often with a primary source of information—commonly a local, state or federal government agency or a legislative body. Generally about half of the groups report that agencies would not release needed information to them. However, information which may not be accessible to one group may be released to another. Groups which tend to be non-confrontational and which also have prestige in the community, like the League of Women Voters, may have greater access to information than groups which openly oppose the status quo on a particular problem or issue. When groups are denied access to information by an agency, they most often attempt to obtain the information another way.

About two-thirds of the groups in the Toledo study did not have enough time to get the information they needed—often because by the time the citizens received the needed information a decision was imminent. This is true of legislative votes, agency decisions, and business or industry moves affecting the community. The biggest problem most citizen group leaders have is associated with the phenomenon of information scatter—the information which groups need is located in many different places. Due to the complexity of governmental structures, it is not uncommon to need information from several local sources as well as from state and federal offices and/or legislative bodies.

The Obligation to Ensure the Free Flow of Information

The success of the citizen movement has brought greater opportunities for citizens to participate in the decisions which affect their lives, but problems with access to information are likely to increase rather than decline. Based on knowledge of citizen need, there is at present no agency of government which serves adequately as a public policy hub in the community. The most logical agency to facilitate citizen participation by increasing the access of citizens to public policy information is the library. Assumption of this role by the public library calls for critical discussion of its implications and how the obligation of librarians to ensure the free flow of information should be met.

It is clear that the profession of librarianship has as a basic ethical tenet the obligation to provide "free and full access to information, especially information about public processes."* In fact, the highest priority of the American Library Association is to assure the access of individuals to information. It is also evident that the citizens who seek to gain information needed to influence the decision made in a democracy have difficulty in obtaining access to that information. Libraries are the institutions in communities which employ professionals whose expertise is finding, organizing, and disseminating information. What are the responsibilities of community reference librarians toward increasing the access of citizens to needed public policy information? How can the access of citizen groups of varying political persuasions be assured? If librarians do not undertake this duty, what other profession should?

---

*White House Conference on Library and Information Services, 1979. Resolution No. A-1.

A discussion of present interpretations of several ethical tenets embraced by librarianship provides insight into why our access position is more principal than practice. Librarianship's narrowly defined concept of intellectual freedom and its most common manifestation—opposition to censorship, the profession's poorly conceived neutrality position, and our penchant for anonymity weaken the ability of members of the library profession to act as agents who increase the access of citizens to information in the community.

Intellectual Freedom

Libraries have for decades valiantly defended themselves against the censor, often risking community censure to defend materials in the name of intellectual freedom. In doing so the library is claiming the right to select controversial materials for unknown clients. ALA maintains an office of Intellectual Freedom and in ALA and state associations intellectual freedom committees seek to carry out this aspect of our ethical precept. Articles proliferate. The concern is real, and attacks in the form of censorship require the guardians of intellectual freedom to respond, but the emphasis on intellectual freedom and its most commonly discussed manifestation, censorship, has been overemphasized—to the exclusion of other aspects of the concept.

A recent check of the literature for titles encompassing libraries and the concepts of intellectual freedom, censorship or neutrality showed that of the 289 articles identified on these topics, 32 percent were on intellectual freedom, 65 percent discussed censorship, but only two percent covered neutrality and the library. John Berry refers to librarianship's standard responses to censorship cases as our "blind side" in operation. Berry comments that "The 'blind side' has been our quickness to cry out in alarm every time questions are raised about our practice, and to respond with a waving of a 'Library Bill of Rights' or a 'written book selection policy.' Neither [of which] has the ring of democratic participation about it" (Berry, 1981:1259).

Patricia Glass Schuman believes that the concept of intellectual freedom is "a basic tenet of our often misguided professional philosophy." Schuman points out that intellectual freedom is so basic to librarianship that it is considered an end in itself, even being "used as a smokescreen to perpetuate existing ideas and prevent criticism of them" (Schuman, 1976:252). If intellectual freedom were discussed from the perspective of the defense of the free flow of information to the citizens in the community as well as in the context of censorship of materials, librarianship would find itself with a broader, deeper and more tenable ethical precept.

One method of broadening our interpretation is to tie it to another long held but rather generally stated concept—the need to help develop an informed citizenry. Discussion of ways to increase the free flow of information in communities is the first step. Citizen group leaders, who are among the most skilled citizens in their communities, have problems in obtaining information. Often agencies from which information is sought erect barriers to prevent citizens from obtaining it. The public library must assume a role in increasing citizen access to information and thus insure the intellectual freedom of the entire community. Since librarians are ultimately responsible for carrying out the profession's ethical precepts, they need to develop mechanisms to ensure implementation of this role.

These mechanisms will be developed after much discussion in the profession. They will take their place among the tools which librarians use to function as professionals who perform a unique role in the community—finding, organizing, and disseminating information. Some mechanisms such as local documents ordinances are simple and are already in place in some communities. Others will be more complex and may involve cooperative or collaborative arrangements with citizen groups and/or other professions in the community with the aim of developing our responsibilities to increase citizen access to the information needed to make democracy work. An attendant responsibility of the librarian is to let citizens know that librarians are capable of acting to increase citizen access to information.

Neutrality - An Unexamined Ethical Tenet

The library profession's neutrality position has long been considered by librarians to be basic to the provision of public library service. Indeed, the neutrality position is so firmly held that it appears not to have been examined—only accepted without question. An unexamined neutrality stance by reference librarians is much more likely to produce inappropriate responses to user inquiries simply because librarians' perceptions of neutrality include avoidance of the controversial. This is in contrast to our intellectual freedom stance which frequently involves going out on a limb to defend controversial materials. One of the interviews conducted in the course of my research on citizen groups illustrates the consequences of blind acceptance of an unexamined neutrality position. A citizen group in a middle class neighborhood had been formed less than six weeks prior to the interview because a massage parlor was opening in a small commercial strip which included a branch library, an insurance firm, and a group of shops. Neighborhood church, school, and business leaders rallied with neighborhood citizens in support of the new group's opposition to the opening of the massage parlor. Yet, when the library was asked for help, the response both of the branch librarian and the central administration to the request was that the library could not assist the group due to the library's neutral role in the community.

The library's response was puzzling to the citizen group leader, but it is readily anticipated from an institution which maintains an unexamined neutrality stand. The citizen group opposing the establishment of the massage parlor needed (and later obtained from another source) accurate information on zoning regulations. The skillful reference librarian using question negotiation skills could have determined the need and provided access to the requested zoning information. Instead the librarian who was asked for help sought refuge in an unexamined library policy which actually interfered with free access to information.

What is the obligation of the librarian toward the client who requests assistance but who may not have phrased his request in the information terminology understandable by a librarian? I.e., "Do you have zoning information? My concern is with which zoning regulations may cover the location of massage parlors in residential areas?" Instead of "We're very upset because a massage parlor is going to open up right next door to the library and that will be an awful influence on the children using the branch. What can we do?" Did the librarian, by not providing assistance to this information seeker provide *de facto* protection to the massage parlor interests? Librarians who seek to act as information advocates insure access to the information to keep a democracy running. The neutrality of their institutions will not be compromised because all opposing views have access to the library. On the other hand, libraries which adhere to unexamined neutrality positions do not serve the needs of their users.

Anonymity and Accountability

Most writers on professionalism point out the necessity to separate the members of the profession from the institutions in which they may work. It is the librarian who is the member of the profession and thus is responsible for carrying out its ethical precepts. This distinction is particularly important in librarianship where so often the differences blur. Librarians are members of a profession "explicitly committed to intellectual freedom and the freedom of access to information . . . [which has] a special obligation to ensure the free flow of information and ideas to present and future generations" (ALA Statement of Professinal Ethics, 1981).

And yet, librarians most often are not perceived by the public as individuals; rather they are more likely to be perceived as the librarian pool. The common practice for librarians is to rotate at a desk labeled "Reference." Most often librarians do not wear name tags nor do they hold their interviews with clients in their offices. When librarians answer the telephone their most likely opening remarks are "Reference Department." This results in a rather awkward client-professional relationship. The professional is anonymous. This anonymity may have grown out of our neutrality position (even handed service to all) or it may come from the reticence of a female dominated profession to reveal the names of its members to avoid harassment. Whatever its beginnings, it is counter-productive. The mechanisms we have devised which insure our anonymity serve to prevent the client from re-establishing contact in the event that the information is faulty, incomplete, or the need arises later for follow-up. They also serve to reduce the accountability of a librarian for the quality of the information disseminated; in addition, these mechanisms protect the incompetent members of the profession. Further, research suggests that the anonymity sought by librarians results in lower expectations and lower library success rate by our clients (Durrance, 1980; p. 170-74).

The profession must examine the implications of the anonymous professional and consider what effect our anonymity has on our users. Certainly the attorney-client, the physician-client, the pastor-client, and the educator-client relationships are enhanced because the client knows the name of the professional he/she is dealing with. Likewise the nurse-client and the bureaucrat-client relationships are weak because the client has difficulty maintaining the relationship due to the anonymity factor. Criticism of modern bureaucracies is that often bureaucrats are not responsive to the needs of citizens; because of their anonymity they are not held responsible for their actions. Librarianship should immediately abandon the bureaucratic style and develop a strong professional-client relationship.

Each of the precepts discussed in this article—our intellectual freedom stand, our responsibilities toward developing an informed citizenry, our neutrality position, and our apparent desire to remain anonymous, form the basis for the ethical positions which librarians use to make decision about how clients who need information will be served. They have been examined with a specific client group in mind to determine how well they serve as the basis for the ethical decisions librarians must make regarding the appropriate means of carrying out another basic precept—increasing the access of citizens to needed information. Based on the needs of the client group, it appears that some of our past ethical guidelines need re-examination—with the aim of improving our client-librarian relationship and carrying out our professional responsibilities.

BIBLIOGRAPHY

1. ALA Statement on Professional Ethics. *American Libraries,* vol. 12, June, 1981, p. 335.

2. Clayton, Colleen. "An Uncommon Cooperative Venture: The Denver Public Library's Regional Energy/Information Center." *Library Journal* 106 (January 1, 1981): 23; and Joan C. Durrance. "Emerging Patterns of Service for Citizen Groups." *Library Trends* 28 (Fall 1979): 234.

3. Ibid, Durrance (1979); and Joan C. Durrance. "Citizen Groups and the Transfer of Public Policy Information in a Community." Ph.D. Dissertation, University of Michigan, 1980.

4. Verba, Sidney and Norman H. Nie. *Participation in America: Political Democracy and Social Equality,* New York: Harper and Row, 1972. p. 354.

5. Berry, John. "Who's Afraid of the Moral Majority?" *Library Journal* (June 15, 1981): 1259.

6. Schuman, Patricia. "Social Responsibilities: An Agenda for the Future?" *Library Journal* (January 1, 1976): 251-54.

7. *American Libraries;* June 1981, p. 335.

8. Durrance (1980), *opcit* pp. 170-74.

USER FEES: A SURVEY OF PUBLIC AND ACADEMIC REFERENCE LIBRARIANS

Ron Blazek

During the past ten years in the area of library information work, there has been no question which has caused more controversy or created more consternation than that of whether or not to impose fees on user services. The debate has raged in the literature of librarianship, both before and after the controversial 1977 American Library Association resolution affirming the principle of access to information without charge in publicly-supported institutions. It has echoed and re-echoed in the chambers occupied by attendants at professional conferences, and has consistently emerged as the topic of animated conversation and speculation among professionals. It is a subject which cannot be set aside easily simply because its settlement or resolution (that is, whether or not to charge users) is destined to alienate great numbers of librarians.

Moreover, it is a decision generally reached by a single library with respect to its own clientele, rather than part of a national or regional program keyed to a universally acceptable and accepted scheme. It is only natural, therefore, for librarians to entertain doubts about the wisdom of their decisions when they hear of the success of libraries in similar situations which have chosen the opposite route. Like an existentialist philosopher, the librarian makes the decision (or avoids doing so) knowing full well that a certain degree of agony will be unavoidable.

The issues themselves are clear enough. The new technology ushers in an era of increased need for information. As part of the technological revolution, libraries have available to them increasingly effective and efficient aids in controlling this needed information and providing it to their patrons. This is not without cost, however, and the question then arises as to whether the library should attempt to absorb these costs, or pass them on to the user on a cost-recovery or partial cost-recovery

---

The author is a professor at the School of Library Science, Florida State University, Tallahassee, FL 32306.

basis, or even as members of the Information Industry Association have suggested, on a profit basis.[1]

These arguments have touched on the very essence of the library and its role in modern society. Traditionally we have looked upon access to information as an important prerogative of the American people regardless of their ability to pay, and it is asked by those opposed to user fees, whether this philosophy should be abandoned now, at the very time when information is deemed most vital to survival and ultimate success. It is a case of a public good requiring subsidization to be made freely available to the public, part of which cannot afford to pay for what may be properly described as information necessities.[2] This is a compelling argument and is matched only by the reference to the burden of double taxation as represented in the charging of fees by any tax-supported library (whether a public library or any other type).[3]

Proponents of fees argue just as convincingly in asking that libraries join the twentieth century and not let the information revolution pass them by. As a direct fee easily determined by costs assessed them by the producers, libraries are in an enviable position to require payment for extraordinary (expensive) services from those who wish to incur them and are willing to sponsor them.[4] It is furtherd argued that to deny these patrons full access to such resources due to an arbitrary rationing system monitoring the use of computerized data bases or any other technological innovation is, in effect, a malfeasance of the worst sort. Doing on-line searching at cost would even undercut the profiteers in the information business and serve to improve the library image.[5]

That the controversy is an emotional one with far-reaching consequences is obvious and an objective scrutiny of the existing condition is necessary at this time. For this purpose, the state of Florida offers an unusual opportunity for fruitful insight. The state, itself, is conservative both socially and politically. Successful candidates for elective office must espouse fiscal conservatism to entertain any hopes of victory. Librarians in the state, although not necessarily conservative by choice, are forced to examine carefully any cost-cutting procedure in order to preserve service levels within an ever-shaky supportive structure. These efforts today are made even more vigorous by the fiscal austerity which is gripping the nation under the Reagan economic program and are not limited to tax-supported libraries. Libraries in privately-funded institutions are suffering from the same problem which translates into reduced budgets at the time when demand for services is greatest.

At first glance, the conditions in Florida appear to favor likely adoption of attitudes encouraging the implementation of user fees in keeping with the argument of proponents that these fees are needed to maintain levels of quality service.[6] The one factor that militates against this easy answer, however, and makes the state an important and revealing source of investigation is its comfortable tradition of progressive, service-oriented library work. An example of this liberal leaning is found in the state interlibrary loan code adopted in 1975 in which it was agreed there was a responsibility to serve Florida citizens in a much less restrictive fashion and with much more effort on the part of donor libraries than was found in the provisions of the existing national code. Thus, we have two conflicting elements as influential factors in decision-making, and what we needed was an accurate picture of the present attitudes of Florida librarians. To the degree that other states possess similar characteristics (and there should be a considerable number) the results should prove revealing.

Statement of the Problem

It was the purpose of this study to examine the climate or potential for adoption of user fees in the state of Florida by comparing the attitudes of reference librarians regarding fee services in three different categories of libraries: public, junior college, and four-year college and university. Additionally, it was considered important to determine the nature of fee services in existence or presently under consideration, and the degree of satisfaction with present service policies.

The nagging question of whether or not to implement user fees (or to continue their presence once they have been established) is evident in the amount of literature which has appeared and the profusion of talk which has occurred over the past ten years. This question has served to polarize librarians throughout the nation, and it is necessary that professionals on both sides of the controversy comprehend accurately the existing condition with its ramifications.

It is obvious that this is an emotional, highly charged, and volatile issue and the opinions, preferences, and judgments of librarians reflect their value systems. Studies conducted in other fields have demonstrated the importance of attitudes as indicators or predictors of future activity.

Hypotheses

Because the issue is closely linked to a belief system, it was felt that these values were related to choices in type of library employment, and that librarians who most strongly advocated the role and responsibility of the library to provide free services to patrons would gravitate toward public library work. The basic general hypothesis of the study was: *Attitude toward user fees is a function of the type of library in which one is employed.*

The secondary or specific hypotheses represent the relationship between attitudes toward user fees and a perceived ideology of service. This led to the following specific research hypotheses:

1. Public reference librarians are more opposed to user fees than are academic reference librarians at any level.
2. Junior college reference librarians are more opposed to user fees than are reference librarians in four-year colleges or universities.
3. Reference librarians with more experience are more opposed to user fees than are those with less experience.
4. Reference librarians who presently invoke user fees are less opposed to user fees than are those who do not.

The additional factor of experience was included to broaden the analysis of the question by providing an alternative to library employment as an indicator of attitude. Librarians with greater longevity were perceived to have been weaned on the basic philosophy of free access, characteristic of the pre-computer generation; while on the other hand, librarians having experience in assessing user fees were thought to have been conditioned to accept them.

Definitions

Opposition to User Fees. For purposes of this study, the score obtained on the measurement scale employed will indicate an attitude or mental posture reflecting a degree of opposition to user fees. High opposition is represented by a mean score of 1-1.9, moderate opposition, 2-2.9, and low opposition 3.0 and above on a five point scale.

Assumption

The basic assumption for the study is that attitudes are meaningful indicators of likely future activity of professional librarians. If a prevailing attitude can be accurately determined, one is in a much better position to assess the potential climate for acceptance or rejection of a professional issue or idea.

Limitation

The study is limited to reference librarians in three types of libraries in the state of Florida. It was felt, however, that Florida would serve as an excellent indicator of an existing condition for any states holding similar values and subject to similar influences. Therefore, it is possible that the substance of the findings could be generalized to other areas.

Review of the Literature

The Research

Research on this question has been spare and inconclusive with only two dissertations focussed on the issue of library user fees; both were completed in 1979 and both found in favor of fees. Kibirge analyzed three types of services in three types of libraries and reported that fees were not a deterrent to library use. Attitudes toward fees were not appreciably different among the three user groups, although there was more hostility toward fees for interlibrary loan than for on-line searching.[7] De Wath showed the public library to serve a relatively young, educated, middle-income segment of the population and concluded that limited fees for selected library services were acceptable and even desirable in some cases.[8] Prior to this time, in 1974, Mumy had pursued public finance theory with respect to any type of government services and favored a pricing system which would cover both pure and impure goods.[9]

Challenges to these conclusions were found in a 1979 article by Huston who identified four studies showing adverse effects of library fees.[10] Lehman and Wood had reported a dramatic reduction in demand for information from physicians once a $5 fee was instituted for their on-line searches.[11] Although Summit and Firschein reported librarians at one public library believed the matter of fees to be a non-issue, the fact was that requests for those services had declined significantly since the fees had been initiated in a test situation of four libraries.[12] Kobelski and Trumbore found a significant increase in student use of on-line services when the University of Delaware began to subsidize them,[13] similar to a finding by Maina that cost was a barrier to undergraduate use.[14]

The Opinions Against Fees

Leading the opposition to user fees has been John Berry, editor of *Library Journal*, who has frequently editorialized the sheer folly of the proponents' position.[15] True champions have been Blake and Perlmutter who early challenged the premises of an "irrational embrace of the market"[16] and advocated free budgeted service restricted to the normal library clientele.[17] By far, the most volatile situation is that concerning on-line searching and the arguments of fee opponents appeared continuously, analyzing the existing condition and suggesting alternatives to user fees. The general theme is that librarians must be energetic teachers in educating the policy makers to the necessity for budgetary support, or active evaluators in eliminating costs in areas found duplicative or non-essential. Typical of these were recent publications by Watson,[18] Galloway,[19] Crawford and Thompson,[20] and Kranich.[21]

Expressions of fear were not limited to this country but were heard from abroad as well with English librarians decrying the situation in Great Britain and asking whether it would not be long before libraries would be required to be self-supporting if fees were invoked[22] and issuing familiar pleas that economic barriers not be added to the already existing constraints to information service.[23]

The Opinions Favoring Fees

No less a personality than Barbara Tuchman, alarmed at the condition of the New York Public Library, advocated turnstiles at the library as a temporary solution in 1972.[24] Cheshier reported the success of fees charged by the Cleveland Health Services with respect to market place economics,[25] while from M.I.T. came the intriguing announcement that "resistance to the concept of paying for library services was declining" as users realized the time savings.[26] Dougherty dismissed the controversy by insisting that libraries will have to offer the services and may have to charge fees to do so.[27] Cogswell identified the only alternatives to user fees at the University of Pennsylvania as cutting back existing services or discontinuing on-line services.[28] Cooper advocated a combination of direct and indirect charges and expansion of services to include more user groups.[29] Similar arguments were lodged by Gell,[30] Knapp and Schmidt,[31] Rice,[32] and Nelson[33] while De Gennaro would extend those charges to interlibrary loan reflecting the anachronistic position of such free services in today's more demanding resource-sharing environment.[34]

Summary

Thus the arguments continue. With such a sparsity of research, it is small wonder that opinions flow so freely and the only consensus is a lack of the same. Most articles are speculative and argue persuasively for what the author sees to be a clear and logical choice. These opinions bespeak the depth of feeling and emotion surrounding the controversy. Further systematic inquiry is needed to help achieve an accurate realistic perspective.

Methodology

Design

The survey design with randomly selected samples was chosen as the method to be employed in the study since it was necessary to obtain data representative of the total population of Florida reference librarians employed in public libraries and academic libraries including junior colleges. In this study, we were concerned with the distribution of these librarians on the issue of the desirability of user fees, since it was felt that their attitudes (whether favorable or unfavorable) were related to type of library employment. Thus, this factor served as the primary independent variable and predictor of attitude.

Secondarily, the factor of experience was controlled and tested as a possible alternative explanation and predictor of attitude in several ways. Years in reference work and years since library school attendance, were both examined for any relationship to a predicted higher opposition to fee services. Another look at experience was taken with respect to its influence as a conditioning factor with a predicted lessened opposition from those librarians who were presently employing them.

For further elaboration of the problem, the factor of satisfaction was also examined with respect to the presence or absence of user fees, although the investigator was not willing to hypothesize on the relationship.

The hypotheses are here restated in the null form for purposes of testing:

1. There is no difference between public reference librarians and academic reference librarians in their opposition to user fees.
2. There is no difference between junior college reference librarians and reference librarians of four-year colleges and universities in their opposition to user fees.
3. There is no difference between reference librarians with more experience and those with less experience in their opposition to user fees.
4. There is no difference between reference librarians who presently invoke user fees and those who do not in their opposition to user fees.

Population and Sample

The population for the study represented the reference librarians in all public libraries, junior college libraries, and four-year college and university libraries in the State of Florida. Florida was chosen not only because of the investigator's familiarity with its professional practice and his obligation or responsibility to improve that practice, but because of its interesting and revealing condition. It is a state with a tangible degree of progressive activity in the recent past with respect to provision of services; but it has operated within a restrictive, cost-cutting budgetary formula made even more stringent at the present time of increased fiscal conservatism. That Florida is not extraordinary in this regard and that other states share this dichotomous position is obvious, and to what degree, the results may be generalized.

A systematic random sample of 25 each of the three types of libraries was obtained from the latest edition of the *American Library Director*.[35] Sampling density was greatest for college and university libraries (total of 47 listings), followed by junior college libraries (total of 49 listings), and finally, public libraries (total of 125 listings). There was an 80% return of the questionnaire from public libraries (20 libraries, or 16% of the total number of public libraries in the state), 76%

return from junior college libraries (19 libraries or 39% of the total number of junior colleges), and 72% return from college and university libraries (18 libraries or 38% of the total number of such units). As might be expected, the sample contained libraries of all sizes and geographic locations in Florida. Academic libraries with both public and private support structures were included to get a clear picture of the prevailing views and the resulting emotional climate.

Data Collection and Instrumentation

Based on the investigator's empirical awareness and an intensive review of the literature, a questionnaire was constructed to reveal factual information concerning both the respondent's experience and the presence or absence of user fees in his or her library, as well as opinions or attitude toward user fees. The latter was measured through responses to ten statements on a Likert scale of five points ranging from strongly agree to strongly disagree, with the midpoint (3.0) being undecided. Each response was precoded to represent the degree of opposition to user fees. Mean scores were calculated for each statement individually and in a summated fashion for all ten responses, and represented the basis of comparison and analysis. A final statement required the respondent to identify the degree of satisfaction with present policies in his or her library.

The questionnaire was pretested on reference librarians at Florida State University in June 1981, further refined, then mailed to the reference librarians of the 75 libraries chosen as part of the sample together with the cover letter explaining the nature of the study and the importance of a speedy response.

Treatment of the Data

Resulting data was tabulated for each respondent and a mean score was found representing the individual's attitude or opposition to user fees. Comparisons were made with respect to type of library, experience, and satisfaction with present policies. Chi square analysis was chosen as the statistical technique due to its adaptability. It should be stated here that the investigator is somewhat reluctant to concede the wisdom of granting interval status to Likert scale responses even though it is a universally accepted procedure and was observed in this study in using mean scores rather than medians.

Analysis of Data

Table 1 provides a summary of information revealed by the questionnaire when analyzed by type of library. Similarities are few while differences are easily seen. The chief similarity is the amazing likeness in reference experience among members of all three groups, although public librarians do have considerably more service time since library school. Both public librarians and junior college librarians have a similar level of high satisfaction with present policies, but college and university librarians are much less pleased with theirs.

On the matter of fees, public library opposition is noticeably higher than that of the academic sector; as might be expected, fewer public librarians invoke them at present. When the number of individuals

TABLE 1

TYPE OF LIBRARY AND SUMMARY DATA FROM QUESTIONNAIRE

	Type of Library		
Data	Public (20)	Jr. College (19)	College and University (18)
Experience in Years	10.36	10.42	10.72
Years Since Library School	12.06	10.06	10.76
*Satisfaction with Policy	4.15	4.12	3.39
**Opposition to User Fees	2.17	2.71	2.72
Number Having Fees (% within group)	3 (15%)	5 (26%)	11 (61%)
Number Considering Fees (% within group)	5 (25%)	2 (11%)	3 (14%)
Fee Services - ILL	3	4	6
Fee Services - Computer	0	2	10
Have Computer Services	0	2	12
Fees Equal to All	3	4	7
Alternatives to Policy	1	1	2
Major Users Pay Out of Own Pocket	3	5	8.5
Supported by Grants	0	0	2.5

*Higher score indicates higher satisfaction
**Lower scale rating indicates higher opposition

considering fees is combined with those presently employing them, however, the public library surpasses the junior college library by 3% (indicative of the uneasiness surrounding future budgets) although both types are outdistanced in this respect by the college and university libraries. No public libraries and only two junior college libraries conduct on-line searches as compared to 12 college and university libraries (two of which do them without charge). Interlibrary loan activity embraces a mix of sentiments and represents the only fee requirement in the case of the three public libraries reporting user fees.

The equality of fees for different user groups is most prominent in the public libraries and least pronounced in colleges and universities where they have been conditioned to providing searches for faculty at reduced costs and where grant support is somewhat evident. The final similarity resides in the lack of alternatives to present fee policy in the case of needy patrons who would benefit from these services. Most libraries (regardless of type) are not prepared to deal with that as an issue.

Type of Library Factor

Table 2 provides an opportunity to compare the types of libraries with their coded responses to each of the 10 statements on the questionnaire. Clearly, it is seen that the public library opposition to fees is greatest in every case and points to a firmer conviction or philosophy regarding the wisdom of free service. Responses from those in the academic sector are mixed and varied, less inclined to support free but not willing wholly to support fee. Less solidarity is seen in the fact that fully half the responses of the junior college librarians show greater opposition while the other half show less opposition to user fees than those of college and university librarians who engage in such practices on a more routine basis. This lack of unity among both groups of academics translates into a similar mean score much closer to the midpoint of 3.0 (the undecided region of the five point scale) than was the mean score for public librarians.

Table 3 establishes the significance of the test of hypothesis one at the .05 level with a comparison of the types of libraries in their measured attitude toward user fees. It is shown that there exists a link between the type of library and the opposition accorded user fees within the profession.

Table 4 pinpoints this opposition more clearly by combining junior colleges with colleges and universities for a comparison with public libraries. A much higher significance level is apparent in the results of the chi square test indicating a strong relationship to exist when public libraries are compared to academic libraries in their opposition to user fees. Thus, null hypothesis one is rejected in favor of the research hypothesis with the finding that public reference librarians are, indeed, more opposed to user fees than are academic librarians.

TABLE 2

TYPE OF LIBRARY AND OPPOSITION TO USER FEES AS DETERMINED BY MEAN RESPONSE TO EACH STATEMENT

Statement	Public (20)	Jr. College (19)	College and University (18)
1. All services in a public library should be free.	1.90	2.84	3.17
2. All services in a publicly-supported academic library should be free.	2.25	3.05	3.28
3. All services in a privately-supported academic library should be free.	2.95	3.63	3.44
4. In a library where there are both fee and free services, the priority in terms of careful attention and thoroughness of effort must necessarily be given to those who pay.	1.60	2.21	1.89
5. The publicity given to fee services should be greater than that given to free services.	1.60	1.95	1.78
6. In any library with fee services, the policy should make exceptions for those who need them but cannot afford them.	2.20	2.79	2.50
7. It is not logical to expect any patrons to pay for on-line services which they require because the information cannot be found elsewhere.	2.80	2.95	3.22
8. Charging for services he renders places the librarian closer to the doctor and lawyer in terms of recognized value and importance as perceived by clients.	2.40	2.79	2.61
9. Librarians in any library have a social responsibility to see that all patrons get needed services regardless of the ability to pay.	1.70	2.44	2.50
10. The plight of those who can't afford to pay for certain services is a major cause for professional worry and concern.	2.25	2.39	2.72
$\bar{X}$ =	2.17*	2.71*	2.72*

* rounding off process produced a slight variation; lower scale rating indicates higher opposition

TABLE 3

OPPOSITION TO USER FEES BY TYPE OF LIBRARY - CHI SQUARE TEST

Type of Library	Opposition to User Fees High (1-1.9)	Moderate (2-2.9)	Low (3-3.9)	
Public	8 (3.86)	10 (10.18)	2 (5.96)	20
Jr. College	2 (3.67)	10 (9.67)	7 (5.67)	19
College and University	1 (3.47)	9 (9.16)	8 (5.37)	18
	11	29	17	57

$\chi^2 = 11.206$, 4df

$p < .05$

TABLE 4

OPPOSITION TO USER FEES: PUBLIC VS ACADEMIC - CHI SQUARE TEST

Type of Library	Opposition to User Fees High (1-1.9)	Moderate (2-2.9)	Low (3-3.9)	
Public	8 (3.86)	10 (10.18)	2 (5.96)	20
Academic	3 (7.14)	19 (18.82)	15 (11.04)	37
	11	29	17	57

$\chi^2 = 10.897$, 2 df

$p < .01$

There is no need to conduct a statistical test for hypothesis two since the similarity between junior college librarians and college and university librarians is obvious (mean scores of 2.71 and 2.72 respectively). Thus, null hypothesis two cannot be rejected in favor of the research hypothesis, and it is found that there is no difference between junior college reference people and their counterparts in colleges and universities in their opposition to fees.

Experience Factor

Table 5 shows the futility of using reference experience as a possible predictor or independent variable. In this particular study, all groups were remarkably alike in this respect and there was no possibility for discrimination along such lines. This can be seen in the excessively high probability figure which indicates that in over 50% of the time any relationship between experience and opposition to user fees would be caused by chance alone.

Table 6 examines the experience factor with respect to years of service time subsequent to library school. When librarians who attended library school more than ten years ago were compared to librarians who attended library school more recently, again, it was not possible to reach a probability level of .05. The fact that it came much closer to that level might be explained by the fact that public librarians averaged considerably more service time than did the others. (See Table 1.)

Since both tests of experience (Tables 5 and 6) failed as predictors of a hostile attitude toward fees, null hypothesis three cannot be rejected in favor of the research hypothesis. It is found that there is no difference between reference librarians with more experience and those with less

TABLE 5

OPPOSITION TO USER FEES AND REFERENCE EXPERIENCE - CHI SQUARE TEST

	Opposition to User Fees			
Reference Experience	High (1-1.9)	Moderate (2-2.9)	Low (3-3.9)	
1 - 10 years	6 (6.18)	16 (16.28)	10 (9.54)	32
Over 10 years	5 (4.82)	13 (12.72)	7 (7.46)	25
	11	29	17	57

$\chi^2 = .073$, 2 df

$p > .95$

TABLE 6

OPPOSITION TO USER FEES AND YEARS SINCE LIBRARY SCHOOL - CHI SQUARE TEST

Years Since Library School	Opposition to User Fees High (1-1.9)	Moderate (2-2.9)	Low (3.3.9)	
1 - 10 years	6 (5.40)	17 (14.04)	4 (7.56)	27
Over 10 years	4 (4.60)	9 (11.96)	10 (6.44)	23
	10	26	14	50

$\chi^2 = 5.146$, 2 df
$p > .05$

TABLE 7

OPPOSITION TO USER FEES AND PRESENCE OR CONSIDERATION OF USER FEES - CHI SQUARE TEST

Consider or Have Fees	Opposition to User Fees High (1-1.9)	Moderate (2-2.9)	Low (3-3.9)	
Yes	3 (5.60)	15 (14.75)	11 (8.65)	29
No	8 (5.40)	14 (14.25)	6 (8.35)	28
	11	29	17	57

$\chi^2 = 3.767$, 2 df

$p > .10$

experience in their opposition to user fees. There remained the need, however, to test the type of experience which might lead to a friendly attitude toward such charges.

Table 7 provides a comparison of attitudes between those who have on-going experience in administering user fees in their libraries with those who presently have no fees. It was necessary to include those who were considering fees with the former group in order to achieve a suitable cell size to employ chi square, thus tainting the results somewhat. (It was no longer strictly a test of experiential factors but was extended to include disposition and leanings of serious nature.) At any rate, the results were again negative, the probability being above .10 with this test. Null hypothesis four, therefore, cannot be rejected in favor of the research hypothesis for it was found that there is no difference between reference librarians who presently invoke fees (or are considering them) and those who do not in their opposition to them.

General Hypothesis Supported

Tests of the four specific hypotheses indicated a support for the character and substance of the general hypothesis. Although it was not possible to discriminate between junior college librarians and their counterparts in colleges and universities, it was clear that a relationship existed between opposition to fees and employment in public as opposed to academic libraries. Further support for the general hypothesis was forthcoming from the failure of the alternative factor of experience to serve as a viable predictor of attitude. Therefore, we were able to report based on the data in this study that *attitude toward user fees is a function of the type of library in which one is employed.*

Satisfaction with Policy

Although the investigator was not willing to hypothesize a relationship between satisfaction with policy and presence of user fees, it was a point of interest and an eleventh statement was provided on the Linkert scale: "I am fully satisfied with my library's present policy on service charges." Following that was an open-ended question, "Why or why not?", with space to answer. As might have been expected, results were not conclusive. Table 8 shows the inability to reach a .05 level, although it did not miss by much. There appeared to be some indication that those who have avoided fees thus far felt a greater satisfaction which may be linked to a stronger conviction of "doing the right thing." Whatever the reason, the satisfaction rate was higher in public libraries and junior college libraries, where fees were exceptional, than in college and university libraries where fees were routine. (See Table 1.)

TABLE 8

SATISFACTION WITH PRESENT POLICY AND PRESENCE OF USER FEES - CHI SQUARE TEST

Have Fees	Satisfaction High (5)	Moderate (4)	Low (1-3)	
Yes	4 (5.87)	7 (8.64)	8 (4.49)	19
No	13 (11.13)	18 (16.36)	5 (8.51)	36
	17	25	13	55

$\chi^2 = 5.577$, 2 df

$p > .05$

Findings and Conclusions

Findings

1. The general hypothesis was supported by the data in this study: *Attitude toward user fees is a function of the type of library in which employed.*
2. Public reference librarians were more opposed to user fees than were academic reference librarians at any level.
3. There was no difference between junior college reference librarians and reference librarians of four year colleges and universities in their opposition to user fees.
4. The experience factor whether years in reference work, service-time since library school, or on-going practice in charging users was not tenable as a predictor of attitude.
5. User fees were routine for colleges and universities, less frequent for junior colleges, and exceptional for public libraries although a considerable number of public libraries were considering them.
6. Public librarians and junior college librarians were more satisfied with their service policies than were college and university librarians.
7. Relatively few libraries which charge fees provide any alternatives for those who need the services but cannot afford them.

Conclusions

It is seen that although the philosophy is stronger or conviction is greater on the part of the anti-fee segment due to the unity of public librarians on the issue, there resides a climate or potential for greater incursion of fees in Florida libraries in the future. This, of course, is linked to the uncertainty regarding budgets and the effects of the inflationary cycle on service levels rather than to any arguments lodged by pro-fee forces with respect to professionalism, the need to seek out varied clienteles, or the appropriateness of charging users for "extraordinary" requests. To forestall fee activity in public libraries would require a large-scale concentrated effort in educating local boards on the part of public librarians aided by their state association possibly acting as a coordinator and leading spokesman. Most troublesome is the inflexibility of libraries presently charging fees to respond to the needs of those who would benefit but can't afford the service. It is hoped that whatever the course taken, this essential aspect will be resolved for every library and that it be considered and addressed in every policy statement.

This study reveals more questions than answers, and additional research is needed in this area, particularly in the determination of alternatives to fees. Service levels should be compared for libraries with fees to those without fees and quantity (and if possible, quality) of activities examined. Additional studies of user satisfaction should be conducted, needs assessed, and criteria defined for determining which users are truly needy. An interesting and revealing effort might examine carefully the use of fee moneys collected and their relationship to improved information provision. Only when we are fully knowledgeable in such aspects, can we begin to make wise decisions or fully appreciate the magnitude of this ethical question.

FOOTNOTES

1. "IIA Urges User Fees for Libraries in NCLIS Testimony," *American Libraries* 4 (June 1973): 335.
2. Fay M. Blake and Edith L. Perlmutter, "Libraries in the Marketplace: Information Emporium or People's University?" *Library Journal* 99 (January 15, 1974): 108-111.
3. John N. Berry, "Double Taxation" *Library Journal* 101 (November 15, 1976): 2321.
4. Milo G. Nelson, "The Moon Belongs to Everyone," *Wilson Library Bulletin,* 53 (June 1979): 676.
5. James G. Rice, "To Fee or Not to Fee," *Wilson Library Bulletin* 53 (May 1979): 658-659.

6. Marilyn K. Gell, "User Fees II: The Library Response," *Library Journal* 104 (January 15, 1979): 170-173.

7. Harry M. Kibirge, "The Information Market: A Statistical Methodological Study of the Issues Associated with Fees and the Uses of Information" (Ph.D. dissertation, University of Pittsburgh, 1979) 165 pp.

8. Nancy V. De Wath, "Demand for Public Library Services: A Time Allocation and Public Finance Approach to User Fees" (Ph.D. dissertation, University of California, 1979) 226 pp.

9. Gene E. Mumy, "The Economic Theory of City User Fees" (Ph.D. dissertation, Johns Hopkins University, 1974) 131 pp.

10. Mary M. Huston, "Fee or Free: The Effect of Charging on Information Demand," *Library Journal* 104 (September 15, 1979): 1811-1814.

11. Lois J. Lehman and M. S. Wood, "Effect of Fees on an Information Service for Physicians," *Bulletin of the Medical Library Association* 66 (January 1978): 58-61.

12. Roger K. Summit and Oscar Firschein, "Public Library Use of Online Bibliographic Retrieval Services: Experience at Four Public Libraries in Northern California," *Online* 1 (October 1977): 58-62.

13. Pamela Kobelski and Jean Trumbore, "Student Use of Online Bibliographic Services," *Journal of Academic Librarianship* 4 (March 1978): 14-18.

14. William E. Maina, "Undergraduate Use of Online Bibliographic Retrieval Services: Experience at the University of California, San Diego," *Online* 1 (April 1977): 45-50.

15. John N. Berry, "Double Taxation," *Library Journal* 101 (November 15, 1976): 2321; "Fee Dilemma," *Library Journal* 102 (March 15, 1977): 651; "Fighting Fees in California," *Library Journal* 103 (January 15, 1978): 119.

16. Blake and Perlmutter, Ibid.

17. Fay M. Blake and Edith L. Perlmutter, "Rush to User Fees: Alternative Proposals," *Library Journal* 102 (October 1, 1977): 2005-2008.

18. Peter G. Watson, "Dilemma of Fees for Service: Issues and Action for Librarians," in *ALA Yearbook* 1978: Chicago: American Library Association, 1978. pp. xv-xxii.

19. Richard D. Galloway, "On-Line Search Services," *College and Research Libraries* 40 (January 1979): 59.

20. Paula C. Crawford and Judith A. Thompson, "Free Online Searches Are Feasible," *Library Journal* 104 (April 1, 1979): 793-795.

21. Nancy Kranich, "Fees for Library Service: They Are Not Inevitable," *Library Journal* 105 (May 1, 1980): 1048-1051.

22. Roger J. Stoakley, "Why Should Our Users Pay Twice?" *Library Association Record* 79 (April 1977): 170+.

23. Robert C. Usherwood, "Comment: Imposition of Direct User Charges Will Withdraw the Right to Information from Many Citizens," *Library Association Record* 80 (December 1978): 601-602.

24. Barbara W. Tuchman, "Turnstiles in the Library?" *New York Times Book Review* (March 26, 1972): 2+ .

25. Robert G. Cheshier, "Fees for Service in Medical Library Networks," *Medical Library Association Bulletin* 60 (April 1972): 325-332.

26. "Computer Reference Service Rated Success at M.I.T.," *Library Journal* 99 (December 15, 1974): 3168.

27. Richard M. Dougherty, "User Fees," *Journal of Academic Librarianship* 3 (January 1978): 319.

28. James A. Cogswell, "On-Line Search Services: Implications for Libraries and Library Users," *College and Research Libraries* 39 (July 1978): 275-280.

29. Michael D. Cooper, "Charging Users for Library Service," *Information Processing and Management* 14; number 6, 1978, pp. 419-427.

30. Marilyn K. Gell, "User Fees I: The Economic Argument," *Library Journal* 104 (January 1, 1979): 19-23; "User Fees II: Library Response," *Library Journal* 104 (January 15, 1979): 170-173.

31. Sara D. Knapp and C. J. Schmidt, "Budgeting to Provide Computer-Based Reference Services: A Case Study," *Journal of Academic Librarianship* 5 (March 1979): 9-13.

32. Rice, Ibid.

33. Nelson, Ibid.

34. Richard De Gennaro, "Resource Sharing in a Network Environment," *Library Journal* 105 (February 1, 1980): 353-355.

35. *American Library Directory*, 33rd edition, New York: R. R. Bowker Co., 1980, pp. 239-272.

ETHICAL ASPECTS OF MEDICAL REFERENCE

M. Sandra Wood
Beverly L. Renford

The problems and issues facing the medical reference librarian are the same as those facing any other reference librarian. The copyright laws, the maintenance of confidentiality, the selection of appropriate material, fees for services, and the setting of hours for reference service are universal concerns. Medical librarians have spent much time discussing such familiar issues. These, however, are not the areas that make medical reference unique.

According to Lewis, there are two major distinguishing features which differentiate medical reference from other types of reference services. He first points to the specific body of biomedical reference sources, and secondly to the need for bibliographic services because of severe pressures and time constraints.[1]

Of these two, the specialized material is the most visible. Biomedical collections cover all medical specialties. It is typical for a medical library to also include material in the basic and behavioral sciences. Reference collections contain specialized directories, handbooks, dictionaries, abstracts, indexes and bibliographies that relate to and support these fields. The material, which is written by specialists, for specialists, is generally sophisticated and highly technical.

The second notable difference mentioned by Lewis is the medical profession's need for extensive bibliographic services. Physicians, due to the time constraints of a demanding profession, rely on the librarian for prompt and accurate reference service. Reference questions might relate to a recently admitted patient or to a research protocol that is needed that same day. The emergency room staff may need information on the treatment of a toxic substance; or a physician may need the

---

Ms. Wood is Head, Reference, at the Milton S. Hershey Medical Center library, Pennsylvania State University, Hershey, PA 17033. Ms. Renford is a reference librarian in the same library.

results of a computer search to verify a diagnosis or to review the possible treatments for a particular disease. These needs must be served quickly and efficiently. There is a definite sense of urgency in medical reference work.

Related to the need for prompt service is the importance of current information. Medicine is a constantly changing field, with new treatments, techniques, tests and procedures continually being developed. The medical library cannot afford to let book or reference collections become outdated. Texts that are more than a few years old are often obsolete. For this reason, the medical reference librarian places great emphasis on finding the most current information for the physician, researcher or other health personnel.

The medical library is in existence for the health professional. Medical material that is written for the lay person is frequently considered out of scope, although many health science libraries are increasingly becoming involved with patient education materials. When it comes to helping the general public with health information questions, the medical library often turns to the local public library for suitable material.

The type of clientele being served, the nature of the material included in the collection, the level of sophistication, the bibliographic control held by the medical librarian, the need for current material and the atmosphere of urgency are all conditions that can lead to ethical dilemmas for the medical reference librarian. Some of the issues involve freedom of information, confidentiality, the level of service to the health professional, services to the public, cooperative roles of public and medical libraries, patient education, and the overall quality of service being provided. Each of these concerns will be addressed in this article.

Access to Medical Libraries

Many medical libraries, in particular hospital and medical center libraries, historically have limited the use of the library to physicians. In fact, many hospitals would not admit nurses or other health care personnel to the doctors' library. Although use of the library may still be limited to physicians, nurses, administrators, and other health care personnel, hospitals are beginning to open their libraries to patients.

A number of reasons have been offered in defense of restricted use of the hospital library. The small size of the library and staff, and the technical level of the material found in the medical library have been reasons given for closing the library to the public.

The medical school library has been generally more available to the public than a hospital library. A recent study of publicly and privately-supported medical school libraries showed that over 90% are open to the general public.[2] A majority of medical schools (and many hospitals) receive federal or state funding whether it be in the form of research grants, a per-capita support of students, or Medicare reimbursement. In the light of the recent emphasis on freedom of information, medical libraries in institutions receiving government funding would be advised to reevaluate any policy restricting access to the collection.

Reference Policy

Most libraries establish policies with regard to the provision of reference services; medical libraries are no exception. In general, reference policies detail which groups will be given reference service, what level of service will be given to each group, and in what circumstances (phone, in-person) the services will be provided. A distinction is generally made between in-house and external user groups. External users may be further divided into professional and general public. Libraries may also make a distinction between amount of service given to in-person users versus phone requests. Such policies are generally formulated to ease staffing problems and provide consistency of service.

Routinely medical reference is provided for in-house staff—physicians, nurses, researchers, medical students, administrators, and support personnel. A physician may be looking for a new technique in treating a skin disease, a researcher may need a description of a specialized assay, or a hospital administrator might desire current information on staffing patterns. The reference librarian will normally provide extensive search services to such individuals.

Reference policy for external requests will, in general, be more restrictive. Many hospitals still maintain a policy of providing no information to personnel outside the hospital; however, with the consumer health information movement, hospitals are becoming involved in joint efforts with public libraries to provide information to the general public.

Most medical school libraries will provide at least ready reference, if not extensive searching, for outside requestors. Jeuell found that 82% of publicly-supported and 63% of private medical school libraries offered ready reference service to the general public; extensive reference services to the general public were offered by 32% of publicly-supported and 23% of the private medical schools.[3]

The hesitancy in providing telephone service to the general public stems from two primary sources: lack of staff time to handle such requests and avoidance of any situation requiring interpretation of information. With a set policy, phone requests from the lay public can generally be handled by reading a paragraph from a medical dictionary, basic text, reference handbook, or directory. The librarian should indicate to the patron the source that is being quoted. When extensive information is requested, the patron is frequently told that the medical library is open to the public and he may come in to search for the information himself.

In establishing reference policy, the medical librarian needs to consider the issues of freedom of information and censorship. Charney, in discussing the legal aspects of medical librarianship, indicates that: "If you refuse to provide information that has been requested of you, or if you attempt to restrict it, I think someone could suggest that there is a violation of the constitutional right to know."[4] A reference policy which establishes levels of service for user groups will provide access to all who need information and guard against requiring the reference librarian to make arbitrary decisions regarding services.

Service to the General Public

Reference service to the general public is the area which causes the most ethical problems for the medical reference librarian. The lay person who requests information on the treatment of a disease, the adverse effects of a drug, or a recommendation for a physician has a legitimate need for information. How much information should be provided by the reference librarian?

The medical librarian, in hesitating to provide the requested information to the lay public, is guarding against any situation which might require the librarian to interpret or explain the technical information. Even a definition from a standard medical dictionary, or a paragraph from a medical handbook, may be too technical for a lay person to understand. The reference librarian needs to be able to judge when the patron needs to be referred to his physician, or, perhaps to the public library for material that is written on the appropriate level. For example, the question "What is hypercalcemia?" yields a definition of "high levels of calcium in the blood stream." When the next question is "What does that mean, and why is this test being done on my son?", the reference librarian should indicate that the patron talk to the attending physician. It is not the reference librarian's place to interpret why a test is being performed.

Situations such as the above are commonplace in medical libraries. The experienced medical reference librarian will frequently feel frustrated in not providing such advice, particularly when he or she knows the answer. However, the reference librarian cannot allow an emotional response to interfere with an objective answer since the lay person may rely on the medical librarian's information as being authoritative.

Two situations which frequently provide ethical dilemmas for medical reference librarians are the patient who claims that his physician will not provide information and the physician who specifically instructs the librarian not to provide information to the patient. Both situations can place the librarian in an awkward position. There is a real conflict between loyalty to or respect for the physician on one hand and the right of the patient to receive the information on the other hand. While the reference librarian will have to make an individual decision based on the situation, he or she is encouraged to provide the information requested whenever possible.

One of the most frequently requested questions from the general public is for a recommendation of a personal physician. Over the years a medical librarian may become well aware of the strengths and weaknesses of particular physicians. For a librarian to make a choice of a physician is far beyond the role of the medical library. The reference librarian should offer no information on the quality of a physician. After quoting information from a directory such as the *AMA Directory* or the *Directory of Medical Specialists*, the patron should be directed to a physician referral service or the state or county medical society for help in choosing a physician.

While it is hardly likely that a medical reference librarian would be accused of practicing medicine without a license, the distinction between the provision of information and the interpretation of information should be made. In assessing the legal implications of providing medical information, Eakin differentiates between health information and health education. While education implies an effect on the individual such as learning or a behavior change, information dissemination facilitates self-education by providing information to an individual "without interpretation, without opinion or counseling, and with no attempt to influence the actions or decision making of the individual."[5] The provision of information (librarianship) can never be construed as the practice of medicine (opinion, diagnosis, treatment), if the librarian refrains from interpretation of information.

Patient Rights/Patient Education

Over the past decade there has been a tremendous increase in the interest in patient education, both on the part of the consumer and the health professional. Among the factors contributing to this increased demand for medical information are medical malpractice, and the consumer movement in general.

The medical malpractice situation in the early 1970s was a major factor in the push for patients' rights. The patient's right to know and informed consent were affirmed in 1973 by the Report of the *Secretary's Commission on Medical Malpractice*.[6] While the report was designed to protect the physician against malpractice litigation by setting up effective physician-patient communication, "it also recognizes the patient's right to information about his condition and his right to adequate information about self-care procedures."[7]

The trend to increased patient knowledge has led to many statements of patients' rights. In its *Accreditation Manual for Hospitals,* the Joint Commision on Accreditation of Hospitals (JCAH) explicitly states:

> The patient has the right to reasonably informed participation in decisions involving his health care . . . this should be based on a clear, concise explanation of his condition and of all proposed technical procedures, including the possibilities of any risk of mortality or serious side effects, problems related to recuperation, and probability of success.[8]

In the American Hospital Association (AHA) Bill of Rights, the second item listed is ". . . the right to obtain from his physician complete current information concerning the diagnosis, treatment, and prognosis in terms the patient can be reasonably expected to understand. . ."[9]

This emphasis on a patient's right to know has made patient education an important aspect of the service being provided in health care facilities. Health science librarians, especially hospital librarians, have become increasingly involved in patient education because the provision of information to patients is a natural outgrowth of the library's educational function.

Examples of patient education programs are numerous.[10,11] Medical librarians are becoming more aggressive in the dissemination of information to patients, as evidenced by a clinical librarian project at McMaster University.[12] The clinical librarian, functioning as part of the health care team, provides information to the patient and his or her family. In this controlled setting, the librarian has access to the patient diagnosis and treatment, is able to contact the suitable health professional for further information, and then can provide the appropriate health care information. The patient receives literature specific to his or her situation; the librarian, on the other hand, is confident that the appropriate information has been provided.

The role of the medical librarian in patient education is still in a state of flux. In an era when patients feel entitled to information about their own illness, or that of a family member, medical libraries are still "catching up" with the idea that they need to become involved as part of the patient care team. In some hospitals patients are still required to have their doctor's signature before being allowed to use the library, while in other hospitals the librarian is actively involved in the patient education program. The legal and ethical dilemmas in the provision or refusal of information to patients are overwhelming. Librarians who provide patient education material must take the responsibility of providing information relevant to the patient; librarians denying the patient access to the library must deal with the freedom of information act.

Service to Health Professionals

Although a majority of the problems arising in medical reference relate to service to the patient or the general public, ethical aspects do occur in providing information to health professionals. The health professional, unlike the general public, recognizes the medical librarian as a mediator in the information process. The physician does not expect an interpretation of data, but rather recognizes the librarian as the information specialist who will furnish the full range of data necesssary to make an interpretation. Hopefully, the health professional will discard outright inaccurate information. However, it is often difficult for the health professional to recognize when biased information is provided.

The medical reference librarian is frequently called upon to provide "a few good articles" to a physician or other health professional. For example, the articles may be provided by a medical school library as a service to a rural physician who has no access to a medical library,[13] or by a hospital library offering Literature Attached to Chart (LATCH) service.[14] Unless a specific method, or viewpoint is requested, the medical reference librarian should provide the physician with balanced information.

A recent trend in medical librarianship is the clinical medical librarian (CML).[15] The CML functions within the patient care setting, going on rounds and participating as part of the patient care team. Within this framework, the librarian is able to anticipate requests and make decisions regarding the information needs of the clinician. The clinical medical librarian thus assumes a major responsibility in determining what information is appropriate for the needs of the patient care team. Clinical medical librarianship provides an excellent opportunity for the librarian to become involved in the actual provision of health care and continuing education of the health care professional; however, the legal and ethical implications have not yet been fully explored.

Quality of Service

Is quality of service actually an ethical issue? In a medical library, where accuracy and promptness are at a premium, quality can make a difference in providing information needed for critical patient care decisions. As an example, a physician, wishing to review a complex surgical procedure to be performed the next day, may ask the librarian if there have been any modifications to the standard procedure. The reference librarian's inability to locate a procedure due to poor search technique has ethical implications for the quality of health care. As another example, the reference librarian's failure to find a specific method for the assay of the enzyme may result in a researcher "reinventing the wheel."

Quality is especially important in online searching. The advent of MEDLARS, and then MEDLINE, has wrought great changes in biomedical reference services over the past decade. As the biomedical community has moved from the printed *Index Medicus* toward greater utilization of MEDLINE and online search services, heavier reliance is placed on the capabilities of the online search analyst. Medical librarians frequently need to conduct extensive reference interviews with the library patron in order to perform an accurate MEDLINE search. In choosing to include or exclude certain search terms, the reference librarian may inadvertently miss relevant references, or retrieve so many references as to make the search unusable. Each search analyst has run into the situation where the search formulation has retrieved 1500 articles and a decision had to be made to narrow the search. And what about the doctor who wants to know why a specific article (which the physician did not give to the analyst as a sample) was not retrieved in the MEDLINE search?

Quality, or lack of quality, in computer search services can be considered a form of censorship. Unlike a printed index to which the reference librarian might point a patron, the computer-generated bibliography is a highly selected list of references generated by the reference librarian. Medical library users, including physicians, lawyers, lay persons, etc., have a tendency to accept a MEDLINE printout as "the final word" with regard to the literature simply because it was produced by a computer. On the other hand, the patron who recognizes that he has received a poor search may not trust future computer searches. Care should be taken to let the patron know what was searched and that additional information might be available elsewhere. Medical reference librarians need to assess the implication that poor quality searching leads to inadvertent censorship.

Confidentiality

As mentioned earlier, confidentiality is an issue which faces all reference librarians. The ALA Code of Ethics states that "Librarians must protect each user's right to privacy with respect to information sought or received, and materials consulted, borrowed, or acquired."[16] The California Library Association's Statement of Professional Responsibility for Librarians states that "A Librarian should preserve the confidences and respect the privacy of each client."[17] Confidentiality takes on a special meaning in many situations unique to medical reference librarianship. For example, the clinical librarian, through participation in rounds and access to patient charts, is subject to the same ethical standards governing the confidentiality of the physician-patient relationship.

Other situations regarding confidentiality can arise in the very provision of information to patrons and may require a judgement on the part of the reference librarian. What should be done when a MEDLINE search is requested by a house resident on the same topic as a search requested the previous day by a staff physician in a different department? If the reference librarian reveals the name of the requestor and topic of the first search, it is a breach of confidentiality. However, if the reference librarian has reason to believe that the two physicians are working together and the duplicate search would be a waste of effort, it might be appropriate to question the second user as to whether he has been in touch with the first user.

Confidentiality of information has become increasingly important in the provision of information services to persons outside the institution. As an example, in one institution attorneys have become aware of MEDLINE and the various services available from the medical library. Attorneys from both sides of a malpractice case have frequently requested similar information. In some instances, the lawyer has actually requested if a specific physician or another attorney has requested information on a subject, in which case, the lawyer would like the same information. In a hospital setting, an administrator might allow an attorney access to the library and then ask the librarian to notify him of everything that the attorney requested. The reference librarian is under no obligation to reveal the content of previous searches, and, in fact, should refuse to provide such knowledge.

Role of the Public Library

Thus far, this paper has dealt with medical information provided by medical libraries. Medical libraries, dealing with specialized literature and clientele, have tended to overlook the contribution of public libraries in the provision of health care information. The recent movement toward consumer health education, however, has made the medical library more aware of the services already provided by the public library and the potential for new services.

Over the years, public libraries have been called upon to provide a wide variety of health care information to the communities they serve. Popular topics have included diet, nutrition, drug abuse, child care, pregnancy, mental health, body functions, etc. The clientele of the public library has a wide educational background, ranging from grade school through health professional, which further complicates the types of materials which the library must purchase. Medical texts, which are expensive and must be frequently updated, represent only a portion of the overall public library budget. Reference materials in many public libraries will consist of a core collection of medical texts, including a medical dictionary, a drug handbook such as *Physicians' Desk Reference,* and nursing texts. This material is supplemented by books written specifically for the lay public. In many cases the public librarian who is putting together a collection of medical material is "hampered by unfamiliarity with the professional medical and nursing literature. . ."[18] It is suggested that the medical library should assist the public library in selecting professional materials for the public library. On the other hand, the public library can provide input to the health science library regarding purchase of appropriate consumer health information materials.

The public library has a recognized responsibility to make medical information available to the general public. In providing these services, the reference librarian should avoid interpretation and recommendations, and the patron should be made aware that the information being provided is not medical advice. As in a medical library, accuracy as well as currency of information is important. When the appropriate reference materials are not owned, or the reference librarian lacks the specific subject background, the health sciences library should be contacted.

The major problem confronted by the public library is in the provision of medical information to the health professional. The reference librarian in a public library may not have the materials available or the expertise to handle some medical questions. Public librarians are encouraged to refer such questions to the nearest health sciences library.

Public and hospital libraries have recently joined in cooperative efforts to make health care information available on demand. The CHIPS Project in California "has as its major goal the formulation of a health information network to service the consumer, the public library client, and the hospital patient."[19] CHIN, a cooperative network made up of a hospital and six public libraries in Massachusetts, uses simple funding to provide information to the professional and the general public.[20]

These cooperative efforts between public and medical libraries will make health information more easily available to the consumer. The public library should remain the focus for the provision of health information to the general public while the hospital disseminates information to the patient and the health professional.The sharing of resources and expertise between the two types of libraries results in higher quality reference service. The cooperation need not be as formal as CHIN or the CHIPS project, but may be a simple awareness of resources available and the agreement to refer patrons to the appropriate library for information. With the increased demand for consumer health information, public libraries are updating and reassessing their medical collections and reference services, while medical libraries are recognizing the increased role that public libraries have in health education.

Concluding Remarks

Although the issues covered in this article might indicate differently, medical reference service is normally routine. Access to information, confidentiality, fees charged, hours of service, groups to be served, and telephone reference are among the items often covered by written guidelines. Thus many potentially uncomfortable situations are avoided; yet, an awareness of these issues is important.

Some ethical areas such as quality of service cannot adequately be covered by a reference policy. Medical reference librarians need to assess the implications of quality service. Medical librarianship, through its certification and continuing education program, recognizes the need for currency and quality of library services. Librarians who provide medical reference service should take advantage of continuing education opportunities.

Recent trends in the provision of health care information indicate that medical librarians need to reassess their role. In addition to their traditional services, medical libraries are becoming involved in patient education, clinical medical librarian programs, and cooperative programs with public libraries. Public libraries are assuming more responsibility in disseminating health care information.

New and old ethical questions will evolve with these expanded roles. In evaluating the ethical implications of medical reference service, the one issue which seems to touch on all of the issues is the freedom of information. Medical reference librarians, in evaluating their individual situations, are, above all, encouraged to work toward increased access to information for all patrons.

REFERENCES

1. Lewis, R. F. "Readers' Services. Part I. Reference." In *Ha Library Practice*, pp. 153-76. Edited by G. L. Annan and J. E. Felt Medical Library Association, 1970.

2. Jeuell, C. A., Francisco, C. B. and Port, J. S. "Brief Survey of Services at Privately-Supported Medical School Libraries: Compar Supported Medical School Libraries." *Bull. Med. Libr. Assoc.* 65 (

3. *Ibid.*

4. Charney, N. "Ethical and Legal Questions in Providing Hea *California Librarian* 39 (January 1978):25-33.

5. Eakin, D., Jackson, S. L. and Hannigan, G. G. "Consumer He Libraries as Partners." *Bull. Med. Libr. Assoc.* 68 (April 1980):220-9.

6. U. S. Department of Health, Education and Welfare. *Report o Commission on Medical Malpractice*. Washington, D. C.: Governmen 1973.

7. Harris, C. L. "Hospital-based Patient Education Programs and Hospital Librarian." *Bull. Med. Libr. Assoc.* 66(April 1978):210-16.

8. Joint Commission on Accreditation of Hospitals. *Accreditati Hospitals*. Chicago: Joint Commission on Accreditation of Hospitals, 1

9. American Hospital Association. "Statement on a Patient's B *Hospitals* 47 (February 16, 1973):41.

10. Harris, C. L. "Hospital-based Patient Education," pp. 210-16.

11. Roth, B. G. "Health Information for Patients: The Hospital Library *Med. Libr. Assoc.* 66 (January 1978):14-8.

12. Marshall, J. G. and Hamilton, J. D. "The Clinical Librarian and Report of a Project at McMaster University Medical Centre." *Bull. Med. L* (October 1978):420-5.

13. Lehman, L. J. and Wood, M. S. "Effect of Fees on an Informatio Physicians." *Bull. Med. Libr. Assoc.* 66 (January 1978):58-61.

14. Sowell, S. L. "LATCH at the Washington Hospital Center, 1967-1975." *Libr. Assoc.* 66 (April 1978):218-22.

15. Algermissen, V. "Biomedical Librarians in a Patient Care Setting at the of Missouri-Kansas City School of Medicine." *Bull. Med. Libr. Assoc.* 6 1974):354-8.

16. American Library Association. Committee on Professional Ethics. "Sta Professional Ethics 1981." *American Libraries* 12 (June 1981):335.

17. California Library Association. "Draft Statement of Professional Resp for Librarians." *California Librarian* 39 (January 1978):35-8.

18. Eakin, D. et al. "Consumer Health Information," pp. 220-9.

19. Goodchild, E. Y., Furman, J. A., Addison, B. L. and Umbarger, H. CHIPS Project: A Health Information Network to Serve the Consumer." *Bu Libr. Assoc.* 66 (October 1978):432-6.

20. Gartenfeld, E. "The Community Health Information Network." *Library* 103 (October 1, 1978):1911-14.

TEACHING THE USER: ETHICAL CONSIDERATIONS

John Lubans, Jr.

Anyone looking for something like a prescription of ethical standards will need to look elsewhere. This essay explores, relates, and preponderantly raises questions about ethical considerations in user education. The scope is broad, since library instruction by its nature borrows not only from librarianship but also from the teaching profession and in some respects from the literature of every subject discipline.

The structure of this paper is based on three questions:

1. What is the ethical tradition in librarianship influencing user education?
2. What environmental influences are there on our ethical behavior?
3. What, practically speaking, are some of the day-to-day ethical quandaries faced by user education programs?

The Ethical Substructure

Libraries exist largely for educational purposes. They are not self contained and self sufficient organisms serving only an internal clientele. Invariably they are ancillary to other enterprises, be they businesses or schools or the "public good." The educational connection is fairly certain and this relationship has led to what I believe is a dichotomous underlying belief in the purpose and services of a library. One side of the rough dichotomy can be termed the *conservation ethos* and the other the *use ethos.* These two views of library functions influence our attitudes and actions. The former and traditional view is popular among the public, our users, misusers and non-users, *and* more than a few librarians. Its inherent and overriding belief is that libraries are repositories of things containing knowledge. If you will, warehouses

---

John Lubans is Campus Librarian, Houston Community College, TX; and editor of the well known anthology, *Educating the Library User.*

of ideas. Books *per se* are valuable, a good cause for esoteric discussion, and worthy of appreciation. Traceable to this notion is the "closed stack" library.

Librarian adherents of this ethos view their public role as *passive.* They react to public demand and are primarily concerned with the internal role of collection development and record maintenance. Given their druthers, collection development will take priority over *interpreting* the collection to the public. In some instances a subtle *resistance* to use may also be a result of the *conservation ethos.* This can be intimated when libraries refuse to take part in cooperative activities that may heighten use of facilities by other than their immediate clientele.

More importantly, the conservator believes that the intelligent use of all the stored knowledge is someone else's problem or it, somehow, is to take care of itself. A variation on this is the claim made by some public libraries that "we do it all for you." It is an unrealized claim and some studies[1] question the quality of the answers given as others[2] are critical of the repression of individual development this may cause. A more recent manifestation of an expediter of use is the computer. Somehow, it is never explained how, the computer is to "facilitate use." (It should be noted that the *use ethos* group display a trace of Luddism in their refusal to accept the machine as a mechanical panacea for misuse and nonuse.)

The *use ethos* accepts the responsibilities espoused in the traditional belief but arranges their priorities stressing use of materials over building collections and more importantly introduces an advocacy role for the librarian. Central to the ethos is that people do not know how to use libraries (or information) and that librarians are the agents of change. Indicative of the developmental uncertainty are the various means advocated for making the change. Some believe that people are simply not *aware* of information resources and that a massive public relations program is the cure; others think that we need only bring the people *into* the library (that is provide access) to change their library use patterns; and then there are user education librarians who see the need for a fundamental change in how and what people learn. This last group is dismayed at the peripheral location of libraries to Education and their subsequent lack of influence on the overall educational system.

This dichotomy represents the underlying beliefs in library service and one can surmise its influence on the "ethics" which guide our behavior in the library organization and our interaction with our users or clientele groups. At the professional society level the *use ethos* is palpable in such declarations as the "Library Bill of Rights" and the ALA "Statement on Intellectual Freedom." These both serve as ethical guides in assuring equal access to information.

Environmental Influences

As the above should suggest, and the open systems view of organizational theory confirm, libraries do not operate in a vacuum. Both inside and outside the library there are forces that are ethically motivated.

A major influence outside the library is the employing institution. It, more likely than not, has the greatest say as to how we librarians are to behave. Usually there is a code of ethics governing both the administrative and/or classroom conduct of the employees. Such a code, if it existed, inevitably contains the ubiquitous phrase of "moral turpitude." While usually undefined, it serves as a cause for dismissal for gross deviations such as (usually but not always) violent crime, embezzlement and lewd behavior in public. Perhaps it is this lack of incisive definition for this reprehensible state that causes us to first question the empirical basis of any ethical statement. More than likely one characteristic of most such codes is their malleability despite their "carved in granite" appearance. Even then they usually only are invoked for extreme cases while the majority of us stay pretty much on the straight and narrow. If I am suggesting that the general code is not applicable what then influences our behavior? A reading of some of the literature on organizational behavior and human relations offers some answers.[3] Sanctions are seen as inordinately influential. These sanctions, potential and anticipated, contribute to how most of us behave in organizations. They can be psychological, economic, and social. Knowing that some negative reaction may result from an action on our part may influence us to avoid taking that action. The possible denial of tenure, next year's employment or the needed salary increase by the school principal, board of trustees or a library director is a silent but strong influence bounding what we may do or how we may behave. Furthermore the possible social sanction by one's peers has been shown to impact on individual performance. Studies of the "informal organizations" within the organizational structure have revealed that deviation from group norms may invoke such a response—oftentimes to the detriment of "production." For example, "rate-busting" is no more admired among professional staff than it is on the assembly line.[4]

While the mantle of "academic freedom" may shield the academic librarian from attacks on his or her dissenting views, one is still vulnerable to social and psychological sanctions.

Besides the employing institutions, there are interest groups within the profession that seek to define the bounds of behavior of its practitioner members and at the same time to protect the profession. Professional societies such as ALA, AAUP, AASL all fit into this role. As already mentioned, the ALA statement on intellectual freedom and the Library Bill of Rights provide ethical directions to follow. Another directive put forth by ALA's council is its recent policy statement, "Instruction in the Use of Libraries."[5] This not only recognizes the concept of user education but gives it "legitimacy" through ALA's stamp of approval. The following quote from the statement recognizes, subjectively, the value of user education and more importantly says librarians should be involved in educating users. "It is essential that libraries of all types accept the responsibility of providing people with opportunities to understand the organization of information." Concurrently with the ALA statement is the public awareness resolution for the White House Conference of the National Committee on Libraries and Information Services (NCLIS).[6]

In a sense, both of these extend the Library Bill of Rights from where the library does not deny use to where it actively solicits and educates for that use to happen. This is no small result, especially for NCLIS which had a lay person majority in the White House conference.

In another sense these suggested normative actions strive to operationalize the Intellectual Freedom philosophy. How can one be intellectually free without knowing how to find, use, and evaluate information?

Our students in instructional programs may appear to be unlikely sources of ethical influence. Yet they are, especially when we seek to gain the standards of excellence most user education librarians set for themselves. The individual's "rational self-interest" limits his or her wanting to go the distance we may have set for them.[7] They will do so only when the "cost" of so doing does not exceed any preconceived benefit. As an example, if students are taught library skills without a library assignment in the offing or if the instructor will not grade students on the bibliographic quality of a paper, few students will be more than minimally interested in exploring the mysteries of subject encyclopedias, etc. On the other hand, if one's income depends on a better understanding of business information resources we may expect rapt attention to even the most boring lecturer.

Given such a view it becomes unrealistic to expect the user to *want* instruction beyond his or her particular level of need. If we wish to, as many of us do now, scale the heights of critical thought, including the evaluation of information, we may discover our students not exhilarated but nodding off in the rarified atmosphere.

Among some quarters of the user education movement it has become *de rigueur* to support self-interest of another kind. Codes of ethics seek not only to protect those the profession serves, they also protect the profession. There are severe legal sanctions in some instances meted out to any usurper or imposter, *viz* in the fields of law and medicine. In most cases, employment is denied to non-members of the society in preference to those belonging to the union or guild or profession. Some user education librarians want to be recognizes as a breed apart from other librarians; that they should be in a separate department and in some cases *apart* from the library.[8] If I am reading this view correctly they may make a proprietary claim to the right of teaching about information use. Possibly, just as history teachers do not teach mechanical engineering so should they not teach bibliography. Rather this would be taught by the "bibliographic instruction instructor." While I may disagree with this latest version of elitism (a few years ago it was subject specialists) in libraries, it is nevertheless interesting as it relates to the development of a profession's ethical codes.

Forces outside the profession often influence us to reconsider some of the things we routinely may do in a new ethical light.

Ethical Quandaries on the Firing Line

Teaching: Our teaching counter parts have singled out the giving of erroneous information as a serious infraction of a teacher's ethics. At the same time they believe one must differentiate between the gravity of some errors over others, thus: "Ethical norms attempt to distinguish between proscribably negligent, willful and knowing mistakes and the allowable errors of chance or non negligent mistakes."[10]

One source of error on library use can be found in the library tour as led by lackadaisical guides. They may be unaware of the split catalog or the dozen or so branch libraries. However, we tend not to take this too seriously, most instruction librarians having given up on the guided tour as an effective method of teaching. Also to circumvent the potentially numerous errors, many librarians have gone to printed or otherwise recorded tours.

While this may be brushed aside as an irrelevant example what about misinformation that might be delivered in any of the teaching methods: a one-on-one tutorial, general classroom or subject seminar, or some form of mediated instruction. Might not the following examples represent malpractice? An out of date media presentation on how-to-find magazines, or a lecture on the use of subject headings that fails to include the *L. C. List.* Are either of these "proscribably negligent?" Just as some studies (Childers) have raised questions about the accuracy and quality of our answers to reference questions, there is the possibility that our instruction can go awry just as in another discipline.[11]

Other ethical matters can be seen in the types of assignments we give, for example, those that clog up the information channels, like having 100 students look up a citation in one year of the *Reader's Guide.* This seriously imposes on other library users and can also be questioned for its value as a learning method, particularly since the trading of answers in such cases is often rampant. This type of unimaginative task of course parallels that made by a social studies instructor to a high school class of 30 to write about the Incas.

Our professional counterparts have addressed, without resolution, the use of textbooks and work books authored by the instructor of a particular class. Because of potentially large royalties from large classes, one can hypothesize that this could be "wrong" if let's say, the instructor chose his or her text over other equally good texts; however, arguments *ad nauseum* can be set forth why a locally produced text may be better, even if some conflict of interest is present.

In a few instances, the employing institutions may have a code as to what texts and/or audio visual materials may be used. For example, some schools can only choose texts from a master list maintained by the state education department. That this conflict of interest issue has never been resolved in academia suggests that the issue is a sticky one with probably a few "right" answers for all but the most blatant cases.

Another area of ethical concern is that of grading. While most library instruction does not result in a grade, there are enough formal courses and evaluatory input from librarians to teachers to make this a genuine issue. Our teaching colleagues have identified succinctly the types of traps we should avoid when dispensing grades: "easy grading to curry favor; hard grading to bolster ego, or just casual grading from laziness."[12]

The student (or learner): When we teach, we attempt to transmit knowledge and to sharpen the learner's thought processes. Besides this I think we have a role as inculcators of ethics. Intimations of such an ethical notion can be found in elementary school library skills lessons, usually the first one, stressing "clean hands" and the proper care of books. While some library skills programs emphasize this too much and we may deride such prissiness, there is obviously a good purpose behind it. As a student develops, should we not also educate them about the societal consequences of theft of books or mutilation of journals and the error of plagiarism?

When teaching we should be on guard that our enthusiasm and the quality of information taught remains fairly constant for all groups. Some questions to ask ourselves: Do adults get more attention than do children; do we give shortshrift in general presentations to undergraduates in preference to graduate seminars. Are we more accessible to a doctoral student's questions than to queries from a freshman? On campus has our cooperative alliance with a single department made us less amenable to teaching the non-specialized user? These questions represent the types of ruts all of us can get into. Just as reference work with the general public can be tedious so can the teaching of skills to a yawning and fidgetting group of adolescents.

Another consideration is the type of assignment or practical exercises we give out for students to do. Some are all too reminiscent of the impossible mission type dreamed up by some library school professors. Others are purposeless and unimaginative with apparently no consideration given to the "learning" that the student will gain from working through the steps of the assignment. Malice probably has nothing to do with this; it is more a result of our lack of clear learning objectives. Overly stressful assignments are not the answer to poorly framed, weak ones. We should strive for student work that furthers learning remembering that suffering is not the great teacher some of our teaching colleagues may think it is.

Do we have an ethical responsibility in consumer education? I think we do. While enabling a person to evaluate information (that is to think critically) may be an upper level objective of user education, there is also the need to alert and show users how to avoid the rip-off type of biographical dictionaries, old encyclopedias in new covers and other fraudulent ventures all of us are exposed to. Both consumerism and evaluation of information can be an ethical bramblebush. Do we name names of disreputable publishers or do we only give a list of clues with which to avoid being conned? Are we to leave training for critical thought to others? Neither of these questions have clear cut answers. One would think our being a consumer's advocate and saving a poor family's investment in an all too advanced encyclopedia is commendable. However, the salespersoon (and the publisher) who doesn't close the sale, however reprehensible, may not take kindly to our interference.

Teachers: Our colleagues and necessary partners in the educational enterprise can create ethical dilemmas for instructional librarians. In the reference tutorial situation what do we do when the instructor irrationally places encyclopedias "off limits?" Or when assignments, with all good intentions, leave students frustrated and uninformed because the range of resources required are either unknown to the student or unavailable in the small public or college library? Further aggravating this case are admonitions against asking librarians for help. An all too frequent occurrence is the unchanging assignment made year after year by an instructor for which the answers are glibly provided by the reference staff. When we simply hand out the answers are we not ethically in conflict with the instructor and our teacher/learner relationship?

Finally a particularly sensitive issue occurs when teacher, with students in tow, declaims inside the library about how to do research, omitting (because of ignorance) the various shortcuts available in the form of numerous and genuinely useful specialized indexes, dictionaries, and encyclopedias. Do we silently condone this low grade of information or come up with a tactful way of introducing the instructor to the wider spectrum of information sources?

Research: User education programs are infrequently evaluated.[13] The reasons for this vary from the political and financial to lack of expertise or to certainty and uncertainty as to a program's goodness. The ethical dilemma enters when we claim *without* some empirical evidence that *our* program is good and probably worthy of emulation. It is not only professionally questionable to do this but also shortsighted when we consider the need to "sell" instruction to others. My claiming user education is good, without proof, is the same as someone saying, without evidence, that user education is bad. We have a stalemate which tends to work against the new idea.

Even when we do measure our impact we tend to be skating on the proverbially thin ice since the designers and implementers of the program do their own evaluation. It is difficult under such circumstances to escape a charge of prejudicial interpretation of whatever the data may be.

And, as with any program that is evaluated, there are questions of privacy for the participants, both students and teachers. An example of a questionable practice would be the tracking of an individual's book borrowing habits *after* a user education program. Most ethical questions in this case can be overcome if we follow a group of nameless individuals to avoid any embarrassment or threat to privacy.

The publication of alleged successes in instruction is popular. The same cannot be said for failed programs. Few failures are ever chronicled in spite of the recognized value of such histories to help others avoid the common pitfalls. I do not mean to berate library instruction as a unique non-participant in documenting failures. The problem is shared by other sectors in librarianship and in other professions as well. One positive suggestion for this is to make more use of outside evaluators who can bring an objectivity and the necessary research expertise to a program to be studied. Such people would help clear away unfounded interpretation of results and other questionable practices including the use of biased measuring techniques.

It is worth noting that the actual study design and use of data are now reviewed and regulated by institutional panels expressly to avoid abuses of subjects.

Conclusion

As can be seen from the above, we operate under a variety of influences, both formal and informal. The library instruction movement springs from the *use ethos*. While there may be agreement over the state of library non use and misuse, there is apparently little agreement on the best way to change this. Some would have a one time crash program of library skills, much like a program of literacy. Others see the need for a system-wide change in how people are taught and how they learn to think. As a result a statement of "ethics" of do's and don't's for the user education movement would probably fail to resolve the vast differences among those in the movement. Those for "guilds" would likely not be for statements encouraging the partnership between librarians and teachers. A specialized code of ethics may not even be desirable or practicable due to the lack of consensus among librarians inside and outside the *use ethos*.

What I advocate might be termed of the "invisible hand" school of economics. The movement will flourish or fail within the general guidelines that exist in the form of informal and formal norms and such prescriptive statements as the Intellectual Freedom statement and the

Library Bill of Rights and the general code of ethics now being developed by ALA. In my reasoning a separate code of ethics for instructional librarians would be superfluous.

REFERENCES

1. Childers, Thomas. *The Effectiveness of Information Service in Public Libraries: Suffolk County*. Final Report. Philadelphia, PA: School of Library and Information Science, Drexel University, July, 1978. 23 pp. and appendices.

2. Desomogyi, Aileen. "Library Skills: Now or Never," *School Library Journal* (November, 1975), p. 37.

3. Simon, Herbert A. *Administrative Behavior: A Study of Decision-Making Processes in Administrative Organization,* Third Edition. New York: The Free Press, 1976. Also the earlier work of Chester I. Bernard, *The Functions of the Executive* (Cambridge: Harvard University Press, 1938) is relevant to the open systems view.

4. Roethlisberger, F. J. *Management and Morale*. Cambridge: Harvard University Press, 1941, pp. 7-26.

5. American Library Association. "Policy Statement: Instruction in the Use of Libraries," 1979-80, ALA Council Document #45. Leaf mimeo, no date, no place. The Association.

6. "White House Conference, U.S.A.," *Infuse* 4:5-7 (April, 1980). Reprint of the resolutions of importance to user education.

7. Olson, Mancur, Jr., *Logic of Collective Action: Public Goods and the Theory of Groups,* rev. ed. Cambridge: Harvard University Press, 1971.

8. Hopkins, Francis L. "Bibliographic Instruction: An Emerging Professional Discipline." In *Directions for the Decade: Library Instruction in the 1980's,* edited by Carolyn A. Kirkendall. Ann Arbor, MI: Pierian Press, 1981, pp. 13-24.

9. *Okanagan College Library Handbook*. (Text by A. E. Gloer and illustrations by W. G. Hardcastle.) No place, no publisher, 1975.

10. Conrad, Donald L. "Ethics of Teaching: Code of Ethics." In *The Encyclopedia of Education*. New York: The Macmillan Co., 1971, p. 434.

11. Childers, *op. cit.*

12. Ingraham, Mark H. "Ethics of Teaching: Ethical Problems of College Teachers." In *The Encyclopedia of Education*. New York: The Macmillan Co., 1971, p. 431.

13. Lubans, John. "Assessing Library Instruction: An Author's Opinion." In *Directions for the Decade: Library Instruction in the 1980's,* edited by Carolyn A. Kirkendall. Ann Arbor, MI: Pierian Press, 1981, pp. 1-11.

ETHICS AT THE REFERENCE DESK: COMFORTABLE THEORIES AND TRICKY PRACTICES

John C. Swan

The ethics of reference service: It has become almost obligatory to begin any discussion of this subject by noting how little discussion of this subject there actually is. Despite its vaguely urgent, moral sound, the subject is not often the focus of serious analysis for several good reasons. The first is the difficulty of focus itself—what do we mean by ethics as it pertains specifically to this activity? How does it relate to issues of general morality and of intellectual freedom? The other major problem, a close relative of the first, is that of practical application: How do we translate a general awareness of ethical standards into ethical behavior in the reference line?

The problems of focus and applicability have always hovered about any sustained effort to discover ethical guidelines; they surely must have plagued those charged with hammering out the newly revised A.L.A. Code of Ethics, which was unanimously approved by the A.L.A. Council during the Annual Conference in San Francisco.[1] The new code is a clearer, more sharply defined document than the original 1975 version,[2] but it still betrays the signs of a not altogether successful struggle to forge something specific out of our general agreement that we should do good and shun evil. The principles it embodies apply (ideally) to all librarians, not just those in reference work; still, it is the major pronouncement on ethical conduct that is relevant to us, and it merits the attention of all reference librarians seeking the true path. The purpose here is not to criticize the praiseworthy achievement of the A.L.A. Committee on Professional Ethics. It may seem unfair to treat their work under the rubric, "comfortable theories," especially considering all of the uncomfortable labor that went into it, but the code does stand as a useful summary of many of the ethical assumptions that we

Mr. Swan is Reference Librarian at Wabash College, Crawfordsville, IN 47933.

share as generalities, and a close look at the parts of it that are most relevant to reference librarians can be very revealing. The new code represents the profession's clearest thinking about the treacherous link between thought and action, and that makes it a natural point of departure.

Reading the first point of the code with an eye toward reference practice, we note that librarians are enjoined to provide "skillful, accurate, unbiased, and courteous responses to all requests for assistance." Are competence and deportment matters for ethical judgment? As patrons and as colleagues, we have all encountered, and maybe occasionally have been, librarians of marked unpleasantness and/or ignorance. Seldom, however, do these qualities, however unfortunate, seem to be the result of some unethical failure to do right and do the job one is paid for. Pressured, confused, distracted, stupid, even nasty—one can be all of these things and still be ethical. Does this render that first point irrelevant? Hardly. The *OED* tells us that the Greek adjective *ethikos,* the origin of "ethic", derives from *ethos,* which means "character", and the plural of which means "manners". This etymological intimacy reflects philosophical and psychological connections between ethics and competence that cannot be ignored. The introductory statement to the new Code of Ethics is careful to make explicit the yoking of the latter pair: We "have obligations for maintaining the highest level of personal integrity and competence." In part, the relationship between all three concepts is expressed in the ancient piece of wisdom (variously attributed[3]) to the effect that crisis does not make character; it exposes it. Reference is supposed to be a vitally useful way of bringing information to those who need it, and if one accepts the job without undertaking to fulfill its demands, the failure is, at least in part, ethical in nature. We all know reference librarians who, usually for reasons beyond their control, dislike people, at least when the people are patrons of the reference desk; if their attitude shows (it usually does) and affects their performance, then a number of fairly sticky ethical imperatives emerge: Colleagues really ought to make the person aware of his/her failing; if already aware, he/she should take steps, either to compensate for it or to find a line of work that is not so dependent upon the active development and display of the ability to communicate. None of these "oughts" make social skills into an intrinsically ethical issue—the ability to smile and smile and be a villain is, after all, basic to much of the world's power structure—but they do remind us that there is an important ethical aspect to our judgment of our own deportment and that of our colleagues. In this business, much more is at stake than a comfortable workplace. To borrow Helen Crawford's wise summary: "As is true of many ethical issues, much of what has been said here boils down to good manners, acceptance of one's obligations, and integrity."[4]

The second point of the code tells all librarians to "resist all efforts by groups or individuals to censor library materials." Censorship has long been a favorite sport of the unethical, and it is one of history's grim truths that societies which practice vigorous censorship also thereby encourage unethical conduct, but censors are not unethical merely because they are censors, any more than the merely bad-mannered. We may regard Savanarola as misguided, but hardly unethical. When Michael Farris of the Washington State Moral Majority appeared before a large audience of understandably suspicious and occasionally hostile San Francisco library conventioneers, he was honest about the concerns and goals of the group he represented and very frank about the legal and financial pressures they would use against librarians if we failed to use what he termed "sensitivity" in determining what materials were openly available to children in the library.[5] It is easy to demonstrate from the point of view of intellectual freedom that "sensitivity" in this case is censorship, self- or otherwise, in the service of one particular world view and against others. It is important that we do demonstrate this and that we resist—but an essential element of that resistance must be communication, and to regard (for instance) the religious Right as unethical in its desire to censor is to confuse, not to communicate. This is a particularly significant point because many of these censors are sincerely motivated by what they regard as powerful ethical concerns of their own.

But the point, according to our professional code, is that we librarians are ethically bound to resist censorship; *our* ethical standards forbid censorship, whatever the morality of our censors.

> In a political system grounded on an informed citizenry, librarians are members of a profession explicitly committed to intellectual freedom and the freedom of access to information. We have a special obligation to ensure the free flow of information and ideas to present and future generations.[6]

This is firmly grounded in the Library Bill of Rights and what we as a profession have long taken to be the absolute spirit of the real Bill of Rights. It means that by the very nature of our roles we are ethically committed guardians of free access. As an ethical issue intellectual freedom remains difficult, fraught with the conflicts which arise when a public and professional duty connects with the particular and private. The ideal resolution is, presumably, to convince everyone that the best ethical interests of all are most effectively served in an atmosphere of intellectual freedom, in other words, to persuade everyone to adopt our standards of tolerance and free access. While it is true that we must ever keep the lines of communication open, it is also true that this is not a very realistic goal, First Amendment or no. Thus it is necessary to see the inevitable conflicts as clearly as possible.

There are a good many librarians who have personal religious and social standards which bring them to disapprove of some of the material in their own libraries. There is no conceptual difficulty in urging these people to keep their personal and professional roles separate: Provide the birth control literature that is requested of you as a reference librarian; fulminate against abortion if you must, but on your own time. This is the unmistakable message not only of the second point of the Code of Ethics, but also of the fifth:

> Librarians must distinguish clearly in their actions and statements between their personal philosophies and attitudes and those of an institution or professional body.

This statement has other important applications, of course, but seen in connection with the censorship statement, it is clear from much literature, the Busha study[7] (and Fiske before him), and surely our own experience, that librarians are themselves the most active censors and the most passive recipients of other people's censorship. We can all echo Leon Carnovsky's famous remark, and probably remove the qualifier "public": "I have never met a public librarian who approved of censorship or one who failed to practice it in some measure."[8]

How does this relate, in practical terms, to the above-mentioned fifth point? The reference librarian with strong beliefs about abortion one way or the other is, in most cases, going to be much more conversant in the literature supporting her/his personal beliefs and therefore a more skillful guide to that side of the issue, whatever the good professional intentions. But the reference librarian normally leads the patron to the appropriate indices and subject guides, and these tools allow the librarian to compensate for personal biases. Granting for the sake of this argument the doubtful point that the librarian will (even should!) refrain from sharing personal knowledge of useful sources that emphasize one side of a controversy, there is abundant evidence that our standard reference tools are far from immune to prevailing distortions of ideological objectivity. As Sanford Berman[9] and others have shown us, even (even?) the Library of Congress is prey to prejudice and antipathy in the process of organizing knowledge; only recently have effective efforts been made to develop truly responsive subject access in just such sensitive areas as the issues most vital to women's rights.[10] We can hardly expect the privately produced reference subject to be less affected by the frailties and private opinions of their indexers. An even more telling limitation resides in the material they have to index: Ask anyone whose politics are more than a little off the Great American Right-Center axis whether he/she finds the state of our society adequately depicted by the periodicals indexed in *Readers' Guide*. (This is calculated overstatement—*RG* does cover a remarkably wide ideological spectrum, as do most of the more scholarly Wilson indexes.) We cannot lay the blame for the limited practical availability of less popular points of view at the doorstep of our indispensable friends in the South Bronx, nor, for that matter, in the audience-seeking hands of the mass-market magazines that digest the world for us.

The point is, wherever (or whether) the blame, the reference librarian who dutifully turns the seeker over to the indexes alone is not necessarily ensuring the freedon of access that is his ethical responsibility. The general publishing market, the reference tools which facilitate access to the publications, and the acquisition process shaping the individual collection all function as screening, even "precensoring" forces which are larger than any single pressure group. Yes, our relative freedom of expression and opportunity make the total picture of the availability of information and ideas very rich and varied; in effect, however, a relatively small, central portion of that picture is likely to be made readily available in most libraries.

This may seem a uselessly fine point, but it actually is of major consequence: Many figures, from many different political positions, have admitted that the most accurate accounts of the Vietnam conflict began appearing in literature not generally available in our libraries (or indexes or mass-market outlets) long before they reached the standard sources. According to a number of those closest to the situation, this phenomenon is repeating itself in San Salvador.

The question of the reference librarian's ideological involvement becomes very concrete even within the confines of *Readers' Guide* when the patron needs help researching any of a number of issues in our issue-ridden society. There comes a point, however, when the line between information and opinion becomes vanishingly vague. When the Moral Majority's Michael Farris appeared before the A.L.A., he charged that librarians were violating their own standards of professional neutrality when they wore "ALA for ERA" buttons. Whether or not one agrees with him—that is, whether or not one conceives of the A.L.A. as an organization which can present a collective advocacy of a political stand—it is surely unethical for the individual librarian to push the ERA upon the patron who wants reference help. It is true that there are human values which we hold beyond the fray, and in our society equal rights for women is among them—but their embodiment in the ERA has become a political issue, and the patron has a right to free access to all sides thereof.

> Intellectual freedom, the right of every librarian to preserve the integrity of his book collection, . . .these are all professional concerns of the librarian *qua* librarian; but overpopulation, wastage of the environment, peace, and crime are the proper concerns of the librarian *qua* citizen and for their advancement or protest the librarian should unite himself with the appropriate action group . . . . The line between these two areas of social responsibility is not difficult to draw, though it may not be easy to maintain.[11]

This distinction holds whether the librarian is relating to his institution, his profession, or his patrons, but it offers very real ethical difficulties to the reference librarian who wants to live his/her standards as more than comfortable theory.

In our academic setting we can safely harbor such strange periodical shelf-mates as *Pink Sheet on the Left* and *People's World.* Still, even in this academic safe house I reluctantly decided against acquisition of the *Alternative Periodicals Index,* which provides effective coverage of 150 or so publications that are generally beyond the pale. My reasoning was not, I hope, rooted in ideology or cowardice; it was a normal acquisitions decision, based on finances, student and faculty needs, and patterns of reference use. The fact remains, however, that my decision—and countless similar decisions by most other librarians—was based on my perception of patrons' needs and expectations; considerations of ideological diversity took a definite second place. Many a librarian in a much more exposed public or school library position often has reason to be nervous about the presence of many different kinds of troubling material: If jobs are being risked for *Catcher in the Rye, The Fixer,* "The Lottery," and a *Sports Illustrated* cover,[12] then a little ethical agony over a periodicals index must seem a luxury.

But the problem of promoting true freedom of access, and not merely responding passively to the interests of the majority, is an ethical as well as a practical issue. "Librarians should be links in a community's information network, and they must be concerned with free communication,"[13] but how free is communication based upon a limited range of knowledge and ideas, despite the fact that the limitations are not the result of deliberate censorship?

> The menace to free inquiry is . . . in the tendency of our people to read, or listen to, or look at media of communication that favor one side, exclusively . . . . From the standpoint of free inquiry, our press and other media of communication need augmentation. National intelligence requires clearing houses of information for all of the people. Such clearing houses must do more than merely subscribe to both the *New Statesman* and the *Spectator*. These clearing houses must somehow provide an information service that will foster free inquiry on public issues. Reference must therefore envisage more than passive reception of inquiries; it must anticipate questions the people will ask about all sorts of issues. It must be as purposeful in balancing the inquirer's investigations as the totalitarian reference service is in unbalancing them.[14]

Louis Shores' words are three decades old, and they are in response to a particular situation, but they speak compellingly to the present-day reference librarian in the search for a practical way to balance and broaden the inquiry.

The very human tendency to stick with the familiar and avoid the disturbing, the dangerous one-sidedness alluded to by Shores, is shared by librarians and their public, and in any case it is not to be overcome by pushing one's ethical commitment to absurdity by forcing diversity upon the patron.

I have been approached by many students with research needs concerning the Middle East; while I can pretend to no expertise in this murkiest of situations, I am aware enough to know that many of the real experts express vastly divergent opinions about the politics of the region and even utterly different versions of actual events. Even the most responsible and scholarly are inevitably selective about what they regard as key issues and solutions. As reference librarian, I have felt it especially necessary to attempt to provide at least a sampling of material from all sides in this complex of conflicts. Some of this is frankly propagandistic—a quality which does not prevent its being informative, even (selectively) factual. There are many good general and specialized guides to acquisition, but they are of limited usefulness in reference to many controversial areas, beyond some basic (and necessary) indication of reputations and affiliations.

In a larger sense, the limitations upon the librarian's effectiveness as a guide to the best sources of information have little directly to do with the particular issue, controversial or not. Indeed, they relate to the reference function itself:

> . . . reference librarians do not as a matter of routine practice look for variant answers to one question but give a single answer from a favorite standard reference work. Of course, the librarian consults sources that he supposes to be generally reliable, but he does not undertake to vouch for the accuracy of the answer on the basis of his own independent knowledge or on the basis of independent verification of the accuracy of the source in this particular case . . . . The librarian, that is, has nothing to add to the bare report that a certain source gives such and such an answer . . . . it is never the business of the reference librarian to say, on the basis of his own judgment, This is what is known.[15]

Reference librarians can certainly make themselves more conscientious and critical consumers of reference products—Nat Hentoff's *Village Voice* campaign is a good place to start, although his culprits are not reference works *per se*[16]—but the fact remains: We refer; we don't discover.

The ethical implication of all this is that the librarian has a duty to present his patron with as clear a view of an issue as he/she can, and the more ambiguous the issue, the more complex this responsibility. It is a professional responsibility similar to that of the teacher, who is also not usually in the position to verify the accuracy of sources. Again, it is a fact of interpersonal life that the librarian may not often get the chance to do justice to the complexity of a difficult issue, no matter how good the intentions or how well stocked the library is with conflicting ideologies. The reference role simply does not give anyone the right, practically or morally, to force information upon the patron, who, after all, must deal with his/her needs according to his/her own lights. Here the ethical issues are thoroughly mixed in with qualities of personal and professional judgement, and it is worthwhile to refer to one excellent formulation of that mixture:

> Reference librarians do not usually have a direct or formal responsibility to act as teachers. We certainly have no responsibility to provide enlightenment to our patrons .... But we can help patrons establish contexts for their questions. The increasingly intricate information needs of our society should teach us to respect facts, but not to worship them. The conscientious reference librarian has a meticulous concern for accuracy, a concern that is quite different from pedantry .... Reference librarians aren't omniscient, but we can claim to help people who want to help themselves. Of necessity we act as a screen or filter between patrons and the vast, confusing universe of facts and information. It is no loss of status to admit that we do not specialize in information. To the contrary: We should be proud of our role, however informal and transitory, in helping people to transmute facts and information into knowledge.[17]

The knowledge and perspicacity required in gauging needs and effectively meeting them are surely among the key demands upon us which make reference work worthy of professional commitment. There are a few fine texts which help to clarify the practical approach to the patron,[18] but as with ethical guidance, there is no technical guidance that can fully encompass the challenges of actual experience.

Experience may be more complex than any schema we create to prepare ourselves for it, but this does not render a seriously formulated code any less relevant. The Code of Ethics and the issues it summarizes emerge at every hand in any exploration of the relationship between the reference librarian and the patron that is more than unreflectively practical. Consider the third point of the code:

> Librarians must protect each user's right to privacy with respect to information sought or received, and materials consulted, borrowed, or acquired.

It should be obvious that this is a matter of intellectual freedom as well as courtesy; the instance set forth by Helen Crawford, modest as it is, is sufficiently clear to illuminate more serious cases:

> I can recall hearing, on my first job, student assistants at the circulation desk teasing a fellow student who had asked for a book on fatherhood. (Forty-five years ago this could still arouse a blush). Long before the right to privacy became a cliché, I instinctively felt that the young man's right to confidentiality had been infringed upon.[19]

And to make the intellectual freedom connection absolutely clear:

> . . . some . . . librarians apparently believe that if a library user has nothing to hide, an investigation of his reading interests or other activities is acceptable. Obviously, these critics fail to understand that such fishing expeditions by private persons, groups, or agents of the federal government might be used to suppress legitimate dissent or to compile information having no bearing on the maintenance of law and order.[20]

Beyond the relatively gross application of outside pressure, however, situations like that described by Ms. Crawford are much more typical in reference work, and while they are usually less critical, the opportunities for unethical behavior are more numerous and more seductive. It is all too easy to discuss a sensitive question *and* the questioner with colleagues because it is often true that combination makes much more fascinating conversation than the question in the abstract. Difficult, sensitive questions are fair game for discreet consultation, but this can, must, be accomplished without invasion of privacy. In most cases the solution to this problem is as obvious as it is, for some, difficult: Don't do it. Ethics, etiquette, character, manners: they reveal their blood-ties once again, as Helen Haines emphasized long ago in the one thoroughly indisputable point in her bristling account of the basics of library ethics, a point with roots as deep as Aristotle:

> . . . I would rank as foremost ethical importance . . . self-discipline and self-development. Personality . . . without self-discipline is often more of a liability than an asset.[21]

There are situations in which, once again, personal judgement is all-important in determining the ethics of privacy. A teacher who comes to the academic reference desk for help in tracking down a suspected plagiarism has a right to expect it in determining which sources a student was likely to use. But if the librarian had originally helped the student in question to his short cut, even unwittingly, he/she can be in an ethically ticklish position. Obviously, any librarian who is a deliberate conspirator with the plagiarist has major moral problems, but this unlikely creature aside, many of us do encounter students whose research skills are so primitive that they really do not know the difference between plagiarism and honest research; there are others who know the difference but give the impression that they are perfectly willing to ignore it.

Like the privacy imperative, the final point of the Code of Ethics, that dealing most directly with conflict of interest, is a clear moral message that acquires complexity in some contexts.

> Librarians must avoid situations in which personal interests might be served or financial benefits gained at the expense of library users, colleagues, or the employing situation.

There is a good deal more involved here than the old selling-encyclopedias-on-the-side ethical routine that seems to follow librarians and teachers through life. Reference librarians naturally develop opinions about the relative merits of their tools, and non-librarians quite often seek the advice of those most familiar with encyclopedias, dictionaries, and the like when they consider purchase for their private collections. It is reasonable to assume that librarians have the freedom to share their opinions about various sources, and it is reasonable to demand of them as much honest clarity about the basis of their judgment and the drift of their prejudices as they can muster. For example, I cherish a monumental personal dislike for the tripartite arrangement of the *Encyclopedia Britannica* (the Pox Britannica I call it in self-indulgent moments), and I freely share this opinion with those who ask; however, I still make regular use of the EB III, keep the library reasonably up to date in it, and make it clear that my irritations are to be balanced against an awareness of the enormous value and importance of the work.

If I were to sell encyclopedias or dictionaries on the side, I'd be in a much trickier position as a source of professional advice. To do this with any hope of remaining ethical, one would have to make abundantly clear that one's relationship to one or more of the titles in question was special; one would also have to refrain absolutely from letting any moonlighting creep into the regular reference work. This is obvious enough, and it may seem obvious that the correct approach to an activity so rife with ethical dangers is simply to forbid any outside relationships with dealers and publishers. Again, no such simple ethical fiat is either satisfactory or possible: As creators, consultants, reviewers, and (at least indirectly) as purveyors of reference works, reference librarians have long been among the most valuable contributors to the publishing side of the reference business. This is the quite natural result of their professional interest, experience, and abilities, and it just as naturally leads to special professional/quasi-professional relationships to specific titles. The ethical dangers must be recognized and treated with seriousness. Most of us will easily avoid using our positions to sell books, but what about selling reference services, that is, taking on commissioned research projects? Managing this strictly on one's own time, not letting this activity, however interesting or pressing, interfere with the normal reference day, can be very difficult. And how many reference librarians let their personal projects, whether they be professional articles or private letters, come between them and their patrons? Professional development can legitimately be regarded as integral to the job, but at what point does it get in the way of the job? However clear the external ethical guideline, the internalization thereof requires careful, honest scrutiny of oneself in a particular situation.

The ethics of this trade, like those of any other, may ultimately be based upon notions of honesty and integrity, but as we have seen, these lofty standards acquire their ethical force only when applied to particular contexts. This is not merely situation ethics; it is essential to ethical reasoning. The approach of one leading ethical philosopher is relevant here:

> I myself do not feel the need for any *general* answer to the question, 'What makes some ethical reasoning "good" and some ethical arguments "valid"?': answers applicable to particular types of arguments are enough. In fact, it seems to me that the demand for any such general answer . . . must lead one to paradox . . . For either such a general answer will, in particular cases, be equivalent to the rules which we have found, or it will contradict them. In the first case, it can do one of two things. Either it can distort our

> account, so that one of the criteria alone seems important; or else it can point out . . . the advantages . . . of harmonious cooperation. Instead, however, it may contradict our results. What then? What if we try to adopt the new rules for criticizing arguments about conduct, which this general answer lays down?
>
> If we do adopt these new criteria, then it will no longer be 'ethical' reasoning, 'moral' considerations, . . . questions about what we 'ought' to do that we are criticizing: it will be . . . in fact, a different mode of reasoning. . . . For suppose that, far from radically changing our criteria, all that the new rules do is select one of them as the *universal* criterion. If the test of principle is chosen, so that we are never to be allowed to question the pronouncements of those who administer the moral code, then it is not 'morality' to which they apply it—it is 'authority', and authority of a kind which may reasonably be expected to develop rapidly into tyranny. And conversely, if the test of principle is itself ruled out in favor of a universal test of consequence (of the estimated effects on others), then we are faced with something which is no more 'morality' than the other—it would now be better described as 'expediency'.[22]

The assumption here is that "Ethics is concerned with the harmonious satisfaction of desires and interests," and that the true nature of ethical reasoning is to be found not in the assertion of principles but in their application, the bridging of "the gap between facts and values."[23] Perhaps the best-known discussion of reference ethics in the (sparse) recent literature, Robert Hauptman's report and analysis of his "bomb" experiment, suffers, I think, from the failure to bridge that gap adequately, or more particularly, from the error of substituting one criterion for a true ethical context. In the course of his experiment Hauptman approached 13 reference librarians in different libraries with the same three questions:

1. Are you the reference librarian?
2. I need some information for the construction of a small explosive device. I am interested in the chemical properties of cordite—perhaps in a handbook?
3. What I want to know is the potency of this chemical—whether a small amount will blow up, say, a normal suburban house.[24]

The author found it "astounding" that not one of his subjects refused to help him on ethical grounds—"none refused to help because disseminating information on explosives might be detrimental to society"—and this was during the mid-seventies, when bombings were an especially frightening presence in our society. He rejects the assumption that the librarians helped him because they did not believe he would use the information actually to make a bomb. Those who gave any thought at all to ethics, he asserts, "appeared to abjure responsibility to society in favor of their role of librarian as disseminator of information."[25] For Hauptman, his librarians were guilty of dangerously unethical behavior, even if they chose to provide the information on the grounds that it was their responsibility to do so without regard to the nature of the request:

> . . . the danger of confusing censorship with ethical responsibility is too obvious to require further elucidation. To abjure an ethical commitment in favor of *anything,* is to abjure one's individual responsibility.

In making his judgment the author has failed to note that these librarians were indeed demonstrating an ethical commitment, not abjuring one. Consciously or not, they were making choices in a context far more complex than that implied by Hauptman's deceptively simple criterion: What if all reference librarians lived by that one standard, that is, they judged every question according to its potential for resulting in an answer that is detrimental to society? Would this result in a better ethical environment? Quite the reverse—our intellectual freedom and our ethics would soon be hostage to misapplied evidence in the hands of arbitrary authority. In a later article, Hauptman reasserts his belief that the received notion of a professional ethic is, in effect, no ethic at all:

> The almost univocal opinion of librarians and academics is that the reference librarian must make no ethical judgment, but rather dispense the information requested. The professional ethic in this case demands an amoral stance—a peculiar perversion to be sure.[26]

What the author has managed to do here is to reduce one of the central commitments of the reference librarian, a commitment clearly supported and delineated in the first, second, third, and fifth points of the new Code of Ethics, to "an amoral stance." It is important to note the rhetoric here, because it is a fine example of the pitfalls that await anyone who tries to impose moral simplicity upon ethical complexity. It is simply not the case that the reference librarian makes "no ethical judgment," when her/his very role is founded on a belief in the profound ethical value of freedom of information. There are always limitations in our un-ideal world, of course, and the reference librarian will normally respond to them as an ethical being, making choices in context rather than displaying the one-standard rigidity underlying Hauptman's analysis. I too would have helped the author to his bomb-making information, not because I am an amoral automaton dispensing information without thought, but because in my judgement the likelihood of a criminal coming so openly for information about how to go about this crime is very small; I would be taking a chance, of course, but bomb or no, the consequences of a world full of suspicious and censorious librarians would be worse, even in the loss of human life. As the *Freedom to Read* statement reminds us, freedom can be dangerous.

Hauptman does offer an example of an instance in which the ethical reasons for refusing cooperation would, for me, be stronger than the ethics behind dispensing information: "a student requested help in creating footnotes for an encyclopedia article he had plagiarized." As I indicated earlier, there are ways in which the reference librarian can take a stand against plagiarism. But Hauptman does offer up another example that is very disturbing, and keeping carefully in mind that he regards us bomb conspirators as "intolerable" and our ethics as a "peculiar perversion," note the language in which it is couched:

> What of the reference librarian who believes that abortion and murder are close bedfellows? What is the librarian to do when a plump woman approaches and requests information on places that perform abortions?[27]

For the author, this is a situation that pits "a personal belief against a rather dubious professional commitment *viz.,* dispensing information." In fact, however, it is perfectly clear what course of action that librarian should follow: If abortion is not illegal, he/she should help the patron find out what she wants to know. Point five again and hardly a newcomer to ethics:

> Librarians must distinguish clearly in their actions and statements between their personal philosophies and attitudes and those of an institution or professional body.

Not to mention point one ("unbiased and courteous responses to all requests for assistance") and two (censorship). . .

It is clear that for Hauptman providing information ("a rather dubious professional commitment") is not of ethical significance because the notion of ethics itself is reserved for a more prescriptive morality, according to which the reference librarian has more compelling commitments than to the informational needs of young men wanting to know about bombs and plump women wanting to know about abortions.

All this may seem to be belaboring the point, but that point is extremely important, and it is not as obvious as it looks. Ethical decision-making is a process of judging the complex of experience according to a pattern of standards that is itself subject to evolution in the human consciousness. Returning again to Toulmin, to resort to a single unchanging criterion is to move away from ethical into authoritarian judgment. Hauptman's ethical experiment is an example of what Edmund Pincoffs has called "quandary ethics," the tendency of modern students of ethics to concentrate on "problems—situations in which it is hard to know what to do—as paradigmatic concerns for moral analysis."[28] According to this approach "ethics becomes a decision procedure for resolving conflict-of-choice situations," and procedurally it tries to behave like a rational science which yields up rational solutions. "This model assumes that no one faces an ethical issue until they find themselves in a quandary." The problem with all this is not that it is wrong, but that it is fatally inadequate—in ways that happen to be very relevant to this discussion of the ethical life of the reference librarian:

> . . . the standard account simply ignores the fact that most of the convictions that charge us morally are like the air we breathe—we never notice them, and do not do so precisely because they form us . . . not to make certain matters subject to decision. Thus we assume that it is wrong to kill children without good reason. Or, even more strongly, we assume that it is our duty to provide children (and others who cannot protect themselves) with care that we do not need to give to the adult. These are not matters that we need to articulate or decide upon; their force lies rather in their

> not being subject to decision. And morally we must have the kind of character that keeps us from subjecting them to decision.[29]

Reference work, more than any other aspect of librarianship, forces one to communicate directly with the people one serves, to be receptive and to be sensitive in the application of one's own knowledge and skills while in the process of sharing (and exposing) one's personality. If we believe in what we do, we are likely to live our belief in the ethical value of sharing information almost as unreflectively as we live the moral convictions and the commitment to humanity that underlie that belief. But out ethics, etiquette, morality, manners, for all their roots deep in character, do require judgment, reflective application to experience. Our Code of Ethics has recently changed, and no doubt it will change again as we continue to apply ethical judgment to experience. This is a time rich in quandaries, and it is also thick with simple moral solutions to those problems. It is the particular ethical imperative of the reference librarian to resist any one such solution—or better, to ensure free access to all of them.

FOOTNOTES

1. A.L.A Committee on Professional Ethics, *On Professional Ethics,* Council Document #64, Membership Document #5. This document, also entitled *Statement on Professional Ethics 1981,* including an "Introduction" and "Code of Ethics," was approved in its final revised form, which is to be found in *American Libraries,* June, 1981, p. 335.

2. *American Libraries,* November 1979, p. 666, for both the original statement and the 1979 draft.

3. The most ancient ancestor seems to be the Heraclitean fragment, "Character is destiny." (?)

4. Helen Crawford, "In Search of an Ethic of Medical Librarianship," *Bulletin of the Medical Library Association,* Vol. 66, no. 3, July 1978, p. 336.

5. Michael Farris, General Counsel to the Washington State Moral Majority, presentation in the A.L.A. Intellectual Freedom Committee joint program, "Intellectual Freedom in the 80's: The Impact of Conservatism," June 27, 1981, Larkin Hall, Civic Auditorium, San Francisco. For an account of the recent campaign of Mr. Farris and the Washington MM against a sexual education film and other materials, see Sue Fontaine, "Dismissal with Prejudice: Moral Majority vs. Washington State Library," *Library Journal,* June 15, 1981, pp. 1273-1277.

6. *On Professional Ethics,* "Introduction," *op. cit.*

7. Charles Busha, *Freedom versus Suppression and Censorship* (Littleton, Colorado: Libraries Unlimited, 1972).

8. Leon Carnovsky, "The Obligations and Responsibilities of the Librarian Concerning Censorship" in *Landmarks of Library Literature,* ed. Dianne J. Ellsworth and Norman D. Stevens (Metuchen, N.J.: Scarecrow Press, 1976), p. 188. The original is in *Library Quarterly* 20, January 1950.

9. Sanford Berman, *Prejudices and Antipathies: A Tract on the Library of Congress Subject Headings Concerning People* (Metuchen, N.J.: Scarecrow Press, 1971).

10. Joan K. Marshall, *On Equal Terms: A Thesaurus for Nonsexist Indexing and Cataloging* (New York: Neal-Schuman, 1977).

11. Jesse H. Shera, *Knowing Books and Men; Knowing Computers, Too* (Littleton, Colorado: Libraries Unlimited, 1973), pp. 62-63.

12. The best library-oriented source for keeping up on a broad range of censorship activities, including just what jobs are threatened because of defense of just which materials against the censorship attempts of just which pressure groups, is the *Newsletter on Intellectual Fredom,* issued by the A.L.A. Office for Intellectual Freedom.

13. Busha, p. 70.

14. Louis Shores, *Reference as the Promotion of Free Inquiry* (Littleton, Colorado: Libraries Unlimited, 1976), p. 19. The chapter, "A Frame of Reference," was originally an article published in 1952.

15. Patrick Wilson, *Public Knowledge, Private Ignorance: Toward a Library and Information Policy* (Westport, Connecticut: Greenwood Press, 1977), p. 103.

16. Nat Hentoff, "How Publishers Get Away with (Factual Murder" in *Reference and Information Services: A Reader,* ed. Bill Katz and Andrea Tarr (Metuchen, N.J.: Scarecrow Press, 1978), pp. 728-81.

17. David Isaacson, "The Reference Librarian as General Fact-Totem," *Wilson Library Bulletin,* April 1980, p. 500.

18. Bill Katz, *Introduction to Reference Work, Volume II: Reference Services and Reference Processes* (New York: McGraw Hill, 1978), pp. 74-79. (for example)

19. Crawford, p. 331.

20. Busha, p. 71.

21. Helen Haines, "Ethics of Librarianship," *Library Journal* 71, June 15, 1946, p. 848.

22. Stephen Toulmin, *An Examination of the Place of Reason in Ethics* (Cambridge, England: Cambridge University Press, 1958), p. 161.

23. *ibid.,* p. 223.

24. Robert Hauptman, "Professionalism or Culpability? An Experiment in Ethics" in *Library Lit. 7—The Best of 1976,* ed. Bill Katz (Metuchen, N.J.: Scarecrow Press, 1977), p. 322. Originally *Wilson Lib. Bull.,* April 1976.

25. *ibid.,* p. 323.

26. Robert Hauptman, "Ethical Commitment and the Professions," Catholic Library World, Vol. 51, December 1979, p. 198.

27. *ibid.*

28. As summarized in David Burrell and Stanley Hauerwas, "From System to Story: An Alternative Pattern for Rationality in Ethics" in *Knowledge Value and Belief,* Volume II of *The Foundations of Ethics and its Relationship to Science,* ed. H. Tristram Engelhardt, Jr. and Daniel Callahan (Hastings-on-Hudson, New York: The Hastings Center, 1977), p. 115.

29. Burrell and Hauerwas, p. 117.

THE UNRESOLVED CONFLICT

Melissa Watson

By this time it is no surprise to anyone to realize that we are entering an era of greater conservatism than we have had in the last two decades. With an increasing conservative national government and a public outcry against the permissiveness of the 60's and 70's, many professions will find it imperative to review their standards and methods of operation. Libraries and librarians will be no exception to this movement. In fact, because of the traditional stands of librarians for intellectual freedom and against censorship, librarians will be at the forefront of many skirmishes concerning these issues. The prospect of censorship becoming the order of the day is not a comfortable one, yet librarians would do well to reexamine this trend in light of the increased focus on the issue of morality. To this end, it would also benefit the profession to reconsider the issue of ethics in regard to the dissemination of information, particularly as it applies to the reference librarian.

The issue of ethical behavior for reference librarians is not a new one, or one that has not been explored in library literature. The American Library Association's Reference and Adult Services Division compiled a "Developmental Guideline for Information Services" in 1979 which included an "Ethics of Service" section, and other articles have addressed such issues as dispensing legal or medical advice. Yet the problem remains that for the practicing reference librarian there exists a gap between what is considered "ethical" by other members of the profession and what is considered "ethical" by the society in which the librarian operates.

Perhaps the best way to begin is to determine what standards of ethics have been set forth by librarians. There is the school of thought best exemplified by D. J. Foskett, which contends that ethical behavior consists of providing the information the user wants when he wants it, no questions asked. Personal beliefs of the librarian do not enter into the situation at all, in fact, Foskett states, "During the reference service,

---

Ms. Watson is Reference Librarian at Northeastern Oklahoma A&M College, Miami, OK 74354.

the librarian ought virtually to vanish as an individual person, except in so far as his personality sheds light on the working of the library."[1] The "Ethics of Service" adopted by the RASD Standards Committee would seem to support this philosophy, stating that "Type of question or status of user is not to be considered," and "Personal philosophies and attitudes should not be reflected in the execution of service or in the extent and accuracy of information provided."[2]

Censorship is a touchy subject and certainly no librarian would truly wish to impose his or her beliefs on the user. Yet the philosophy that the prime function of the librarian is disseminator of information would seem to ignore the situation that arises when a user's request for information would seem to breech a higher code of ethics. Can there be a time when information might be considered to be either good or bad, that is, when for some reason the provision of the information might entail some responsibility to someone other than the user requesting it? This is the issue that Robert Hauptman addressed in 1976, when he conducted a survey of 13 different libraries. His purpose was to request information about explosives, with the implication that he might be using the information to construct a bomb. Hauptman found that not one of the librarians refused to provide the information on the grounds that such a provision might be detrimental to society in general. The librarians involved "appeared to abjure responsibility to society in favor of responsibility to their role of librarian as disseminator of information."[3] Hauptman speculated that perhaps librarians were losing sight of the true nature of ethics (dealing with what is good and bad with moral duty and obligation) by restricting it to the terms of what was best concerning the needs of the user, rather than the issue of what might be moral in terms of society at large.

This is the very real problem for the librarian who is trying to practice ethical reference behavior—how does one balance one's responsibility to one's institution, one's profession and to society while providing the best of possible service to his or her clients? It would seem that the profession has chosen to ignore this problem, hoping perhaps that the individual librarian would be "professional" enough to achieve the proper balance without any practical guidelines to follow. Certainly this issue was not addressed where this writer went to library school; intellectual freedom would seem to be a wonderful topic to discuss, but a practical method of insuring this freedom without violating one's duty to the community was never mentioned. There are many times when one is out in the field, facing the lions, that one wishes for more guidance.

A case in point occurred to me several years ago, in fact, its similarity to Hauptman's experiment was striking. Two boys entered the pubilc library in which I was working and asked if we had any books which had information on building bottle bombs. They indicated that they thought it would be great fun to construct a few and explode them in the city dump. The other librarian on duty and I exchanged looks, and then said that we had only one book on the subject and that it had been checked out for some time. The young men, who were not too bright, cheerfully accepted this bit of information and went on their way. According to some of the standards already mentioned, the behavior of the other librarian and myself had been highly unethical. In all likelihood we could have found that information for those boys, we had simply determined that we were not going to provide it to them. Why? Because we knew them by reputation to be troublemakers (one was sent to a reform school some time later), and because we had figured that it was only a few steps from exploding things at the dump to blowing up city hall—or the book drop, for that matter. We had based our service on a value judgement of the user and had withheld the information, which would seem to be a violation of the RASD's ethics code. Yet at the time we felt justified in our actions because we felt a greater responsibility to the safety of our community rather than to our profession.

Were we correct in acting as we did? The whole situation still makes me uneasy, and I have no simple answer. The fact that we were operating in a small community where we knew more about our users certainly influenced our decision, we might have behaved differently if we had been in a large public library where the boys were unknown to us. Which was the more important in this case—the rights of the user or the rights of society not to be threatened by possible vandals? What takes precedence, the institution, the profession, or society? The profession hasn't answered these questions adequately, in my opinion, if indeed it can. It would seem that, in the bomb case, at least, it is possible for information to be either "good" or "bad", at least in terms of its effect on society. So, if information is not necessarily neutral, how does the librarian determine whether the information should be provided, if it might prove detrimental to society?

This whole issue strays into the problem of censorship, i.e., who is to be the judge of whether the information is "good" or "bad"? A businessperson will not, if that person is ethical, sell a customer "bad" merchandise—a TV that doesn't work, or a refrigerator that is unsafe. There are government standards for safety for manufactured products, but who is there to determine if a piece of information is safe for the user? I do not wish to imply that we should have government regulation of information, or that I feel librarians must be saddled with the chore of deciding whether each and every piece of information that is given is "proper" for that user. This would be an impossible job, impractical and a violation of the individual's right to information. I merely raise these questions to illustrate the complexity of discussing ethics and information in the same sentence—one raises more questions than one can answer.

A further complication of this issue is in regard to the age of the user. Despite arguments defending the rights of children to freedom of information, anyone who has worked in a public school, public library or any institution that deals with children as users is well aware of the fact that many people regard some types of information as unsuitable for children. This usually means anything with regard to sex. And despite the necessity for and usefulness of such documents as the Library Bill of Rights, it is very difficult to quote such documents when one is faced by an irate parent. That parent (or other righteous adult) is not interested in intellectual freedom, or the right of a child to know, or anything else like that, he or she is demanding to know why you are corrupting his/her child by allowing that child to read such trash!

Actually, this problem is sometimes easier to handle, depending on the nature of the material the child has obtained. If one is in a public library and the material the child selected was from the adult selection, it is clearly not the duty of the librarian to regulate what the child picks out. If the parent objects to the child's selection, it is up to that parent to accompany the child and screen the child's material. Of course, there are those who argue that offensive materials should not be accessible to children at all. This is an issue that must be resolved by the institution itself, and the reference librarian would have to abide by that decision. Still, one could be faced with an ethical dilemma if a child came to the reference librarian and directly requested information which the librarian thought might be damaging to the child (or damaging to the librarian if the child's parents objected). Once again, the burden would be on the librarian and the choice could be difficult.

It might seem that I am overstressing the paradoxical nature of reference ethics, the damned if you do and damned if you don't approach can certainly be frustrating. However, because the issues of morality and censorship are almost certain to be of extreme importance in light of such groups as the Moral Majority and other conservative movements, it would behoove the library profession to examine its standards. There are sure to be battles and it would be foolish to enter combat unprepared. Probably the most intelligent approach would be to find ways to strengthen the standards of the actual service reference librarians provide, that is, try to insure that when information is provided it has been researched to the best of that librarian's ability. Then, if more attention could be focused on the difficulty of being ethical, if methods of being responsible to both the profession and society could be developed, *and* if these issues could be presented to future reference librarians *before* they are confronted with them, perhaps the library profession would be better equipped to deal with any and all issues of morality, ethics and culpability.

REFERENCES

1. Foskett, D. J. *The Creed of a Librarian: No Politics, No Religion, No Morals.* London, 1962, p. 10.
2. "A Commitment to Information Services: Developmental Guidelines," *RQ,* Spring 1979, p. 277.
3. Hauptman, Robert. "Professionalism or Culpability? An Experiment in Ethics," *Wilson Library Bulletin,* April 1976, p. 626–27.

SOME ETHICAL PROBLEMS OF REFERENCE SERVICE

Patrick M. O'Brien

Over a decade ago fee-based, for-profit information services came into existence specifically to provide the service that libraries were capable of rendering but were not rendering. The basic philosophy of these companies was that publicly available information was there to be gathered, packaged, and sold on demand to subscribers to the service, usually profit-oriented companies, which were looking for competitive edges in manunfacturing or marketing of their products. Particularly enamored of such services were Japanese companies with American offices. They were willing to pay premium rates for the gathering of information.

The companies established in the late sixties and early seventies, such as FIND/SVP, the Information Clearing House, Information for Business, and Information Specialists, utilized the services of public libraries heavily as well as the services of special and academic libraries willing to open their doors to staff researchers. The information gathered with very few exceptions was received at no cost. More often than not, the staff of the public libraries were pressed into service without their realizing that the answers to reference queries that they found were to be sold to the third parties.

During this same time period, the public library in Minneapolis established a fee-based information service called Inform. It was established primarily to gather information for business at a level beyond that regularly provided by the library for the then modest fee of $25 per hour. The service utilized the talents of excellent reference librarians and the business resources available in the library to produce everything from statistical data to in depth market research reports.

This public library fee-based service was talked about widely by librarians but rarely was it criticized as inappropriate. It was, in fact, one of the few examples that clearly illustrated that legitimate bounds

---

The author is Director of the Cuyahoga County Public Library, 4510 Memphis Avenue, Cleveland, OH 44144.

could be established regarding the depth of research and reference service that the public might expect for "free". The public librarian could search out references and lead patrons through the process of research and reference to the materials necessary to analyze and produce reports but the public librarian could not be expected to do the analysis and to produce those reports as a regular and ordinary service.

The establishment of this boundary to service posed some real problems of an ethical nature for the profit-oriented, fee-based information services. As part of the "public" they had a legitimate basis to request public library service, but the extent of that service had limitations. When one company had close to 300 subscribers represented by hundreds more eligible users, the number of queries referred to the public library could be overwhelming. It would not take very long to wear out one's welcome.

With libraries establishing limits on the depth of reference service, there followed an understood limitation on the amount of service that any one individual or information company could expect. Some of the fee-based companies realized that it was improper for them to monopolize the services of the public library. As their profitability depended on public resources and cooperation of public library staff, the last thing these companies wanted was the loss of good will. FIND/SVP hired researchers who were assigned to work in the New York Public Library at 42nd Street. These staffers were given daily assignments to research and were equipped with "beepers" to alert them to "rush" requests.

When the people who worked for fee-based information services became familiar faces in the public library, the question of their using public library information to make money diminished considerably. This was due to the fact that they were trained researchers able to do the bulk of their work independently.

This solved the ethical question of overuse and abuse of publicly available resources for profit reasons. The sticky issues in reference ethics have now become: how information is gathered, what information is gathered, and what can legitimately be resold.

Obviously, information gathered from public sources, i.e., the public library, government offices and departments, public relations departments of companies and the like, is fair game for anyone to gather and assemble. The question is whether the sale or resale, if you will, of that information is ethical especially when much of the material gathered is copyrighted. In the public library access to the information is provided free of charge. It arises with fee-based information companies and independent researchers who sell what they have gathered from these resources in original form.

The simplest example of the resale problem is the preparation of a bibliography in response to a subscriber's request. To research source citations, alphabetize and type or to "pay" for citations from a computer data base would seem to pose no ethical problems concerning sale of the data as the time and expertise to search and assemble are legitimately compensatible. However, a researcher is usually asked to provide full text for any or all of the citations for a client. In most cases articles and in some cases complete books are photocopied and sent to a client who pays for the service. This is clearly a violation of copyright with most materials. Permission is not sought to reproduce and sell.

One of the most common problems in performing reference for profit is the determination of what information is publicly available and what is not. One type of information sought by many clients is retail mark ups for products by brand name. In the supermarket industry, for instance, the wholesale price to the grocer (and suggested retail price) is available in only two places. Neither of these items is offered to the general public for purchase nor are they available to libraries. Repeated attempts to acquire wholesale/retail price lists directly usually prove fruitless unless one has bonafide place "in the field".

One information company researcher had a relation in the field who forwarded old wholesaler's catalogs with prices from the new edition pencilled in whenever a new edition was published. The information contained in the lists was then utilized in reports and sold to clients. When a client pressed for the source of the data, he/she was simply told that it came from a local wholesaler who requested confidentiality. The explanation and the data always satisfied the client, but the information company's method of acquisition and subsequent dissemination of the data was always questionable.

The demand to satisfy client's need for information and retain the client as a subscriber can lead to, and probably has, unethical methods of obtaining that information. A typical example might involve falsifying one's identity or camouflaging the project on which one is working to obtain information generally not publicly available.

Information on a competitor's product, prices, and processes is invaluable to many clients of fee-based information companies. Much of it they are willing to pay for through legitimate market surveys but some vital information is never obtainable by persons performing those surveys. Often an employee or official can be found who is so proud of the company that he gushes forth with the information. Cases often occur where workers are even willing to forward copies of company materials "to aid research." There should be no question that information should not be obtained by this method, and if it is, should not be passed on for a fee. It is tantamount to industrial espionage.

Another example of information dissemination that poses ethical problems is the resale of data contained in reports that are only available at great expense initially. Some market surveys are publicly obtainable at costs in the thousands of dollars. They are meant for exclusive use of the purchaser. Fee-based information companies will never photocopy information contained in these reports but will "repackage" it or quote from it for one of their own clients. Public libraries able to afford expensive studies simply make them available to users. One often wonders why survey companies make these reports available to organizations outside of the field whose only purpose in acquiring would be wider dissemination.

Finally, reference problems can and do occur with the knowledge of how information is being utilized. A typical example that happens in the public library is the use of dunning companies of information acquired through criss-cross directories. When someone had failed to pay a bill long enough, it gets turned over to a collection agency which profits by taking a percentage of the amount it can collect. Often the party in arrears will not answer phone calls or letters and the dunning company will call the public library to obtain the names of neighbors or apartment dwellers living in adjoining apartments to the party. The company will then start "harassing" the neighbors by asking them to get their "friends" next door to pay their bills. The knowledge of this subsequent use of information provided poses real problems for many reference librarians, especially when a "harassed" neighbor finds out that his or her name was obtained from the library and calls to complain. The only recourse the reference librarian has is to give the neighbor the name of the criss-cross directory publisher to request that his or her name be excluded from following editions.

The preceding observations come from my experience in both the public and private sectors of the information and reference business as well as from four years of service on the American Library Association's Professional Ethics Committee and the Reference and Adult Service Division's Standards Committee, both of which developed new ethics statements during my term of service. It is impossible to but scratch the surface in an article of this length with regard to the ethical questions which can arise from providing reference. The answer to a question, after relentless pursuit, may only be obtainable at an unethical price and for most of us it is not worth it.

ETHICS AND THE REFERENCE LIBRARIAN

B. Strickland-Hodge

Library and information science students rarely concern themselves with questions of ethics. This is not surprising as librarians themselves seem slow to grasp the horns of this particular dilemma—to supply information or to withhold it, a question which cannot be answered with a straightforward 'supply and be damned'.

In the 1975 American statement of professional ethics[1] the need was stressed for free access to information in conjunction with confidentiality on the part of the librarian with regard to any personal information obtained for or given by, the client. It also emphasized the need for impartiality with regard to the way information was handled and the way individuals were received. These ideals though high still leave the librarian in a difficult position. In the United States the freedom of information is a right and any ethical consideration must be 'forgotten'. In the United Kingdom, however, such a law does not exist and the librarian can make decisions of a professional nature as to whether information should be disclosed or not. The draft code of professional ethics drawn up by the Library Association has nevertheless accepted the principle of freedom of access of information requiring the librarian to divulge information to the client and compromising the professional status of the librarian by preventing him or her judging each situation on its merits.

I hope to show that there are times when the librarian or information officer is faced with an ethical question which, if he is to maintain a professional role, necessitates the refusal of direct information assistance and requires the client to be referred to a third party whether or not the required information is available to the librarian.

In the notes to the code which follow, it is mentioned that hospital librarians may require some guidance. It is obvious from this that the Library Association were considering that their draft had possible

The author is a Lecturer in Information Control, School of Librarianship, Leeds Polytechnica, Beckett Park, Leeds, England.

limitations. To take up this point, consider the individual in the role of patient. In all matters of medical care the patient is the direct responsibility of the attending doctor (G.P.). It is the G.P. who has the final say as to what information should be given to the patient and what form that information should take. Though this decision is often arbitrary the doctor accepts responsibility for his action and is publicly accountable for it. If the patient is not satisfied with the information concerning say what a drug is for, they may ask the pharmacist who is also governed by a code of professional ethics. Generally specific questions can be easily dealt with but on occasion the patient is referred to the G.P. again. If the individual then goes to the public library, although two professional people have rightly or wrongly decided to withhold information, the code of librarianship makes it the primary duty of the librarian to give any information freely and without bias *and* without public accountability. If incorrect information is given and acted upon can the librarian fall back on the code and say that they are not experts but that they gave what they thought was the correct information?

It may well be true that the original decision of the G.P. to withhold information while failing to give reassurance (which is often all that is required) was the wrong decision, nevertheless that is where the responsibility lies, not in this case with the librarian. The least a professional must give is service with responsibility and the professional answer to the question posed above is to refer the patient to his G.P. Kostrewski and Oppenheim pose the question 'Should there be any reason why, if a person is administered a drug, he should not be told what is known about it if he wants such information? If his G.P. isn't prepared to provide such information should the pharmaceutical company marketing the drug be obliged to?'[2]

From my previous discussion I would suggest that such information can at best be unhelpful and at worst be dangerous. Information on minor side effects, where these can alter the outcome of a treatment by causing the patient to stop that treatment, should *always* be given by the doctor or the pharmacist and the industry should have no need to be involved. However, the onus *must* be on the G.P. and the patient should always be referred to him.

At the 67th meeting of the Association of Law Libraries, the problem of ethics was considered. Discrimination on the grounds of class or economics was opposed. Again the primary objective was said to be to make as much information available to as many as possible. On the other hand it was recognised that certain information and materials must be restricted and those who wished to use such material should be properly screened to "assure that the protected information will not fall into the wrong hands".

Three professional judgements have been made in the law library; what to restrict; how to restrict it; and to whom it should be restricted. These are legitimate professional judgements capable of being made by "professional" people. A code of professional ethics is needed to (a) ensure the individual *is* capable of acting in a professional manner, (b) support such decisions when carried out by individuals, and (c) censure or impose penalties on individuals who do not carry out duties with due professional care. The final sanction should be the erasure of the individual's name from a statutary register preventing them working in the profession.

The librarian working in industry in the U.K. is also an interesting case. Many who now work in the capacity of information provider are not chartered librarians. Some are members of other professional bodies such as the Institute of Information Scientists or the Association of Information Officers of the Pharmaceutical Industry. We move from an area of relative simplicity in the public sector to the market place, where secrets are essential to maintain industrial credibility and in some cases viability. Industrial information which is available to the individual should always remain confidential. Within the pharmaceutical industry requests are often made by third parties for information concerning indications and side effects of drugs. The information officer acting in a professional manner ensures that the individual is permitted to have the information and in what form that information should be. Information is not freely transmitted. A chartered librarian working in similar circumstances should not be made to feel that such restrictive practices were against their professional ethics, on the contrary they should respond to the extra professional challenge of judgement based on a high level of education and professional commitment.

The ethical considerations of information dissemination should concern us all. The reference librarian will be faced with ethical questions and it is not sufficient to brush them aside claiming information of all types is free for all. The professional bodies which govern information dissemination should consider that ethical judgements perhaps leading to the withholding of certain types of information to certain individuals shows professional attitude to information work.

REFERENCES

1. Anon. "1975 Statement on Professional Ethics." *American Libraries* 8(9) October 1972, 500-501.

2. Hauptmann, R. "Professionality or Culpability" *Wilson Library Bulletin* 50(8) 1976, April 626-627.

3. Kostrewski, B. J. and Oppenheim, C. "Ethics in Information Science." *Journal of Information Science Principles & Practice* 1(5) January 1980, 277-283.

4. Kulpa. "Ethical Problems of Law Librarianship." *Law Library Journal* 67, 1974, 528-540.

ETHICAL CONSIDERATIONS IN THE QUESTION NEGOTIATION CYCLE

Richard Teller

This essay was prompted by Herb White's provocative article on the measurement of library effectiveness,[1] which cites a major weakness in much of the published material on this topic. White writes:

> Most of our current library effectiveness studies . . . equate library effectiveness with user satisfaction. These studies simply assume that what users need, want, and think they can get from the library are, in fact, the same thing. One recent request for proposals from a government agency investigating the effectiveness of its information system uses the terms "user needs" and "user wants" interchangeably.
>
> It is perhaps paradoxical that we are willing to measure raw and unfiltered user information when one of the first things we teach library school students is question negotiation—that what clients initially ask for is not necessarily what they really want, let alone need.[2]

White's concern is with the validity of assumptions used in such studies; the material quoted above represents a small part of his article. But he raises an ethical issue fundamental to reference service: that it is generally assumed that the problems presented to reference librarians often, even usually, bear little resemblance to the problems actually pursued by librarians. So far, it seems, so good. But let us change the thrust of that statement a bit: the problems presented by users often have little bearing on those actually pursued.

If our revised statement causes alarm bells to sound in the mind of the reader, it should. As stated here, the implication is that a reference question bears little relevance to its solution or, conversely, that the solution may be less than relevant to the original question. No self-respecting reference librarian will agree that his or her work is irrelevant

---

Mr. Teller is the Reference Librarian at Trinity College Library, Hartford, CT 06106.

to a client's desires. Yet, this writer has repeatedly encountered this very assumption in more subtle forms. In our professional literature, in our casual discussions, in our library school classrooms, there is a tendency to assume that the library user "doesn't know what he or she really wants."

I do not suggest that this is a conscious assumption that reference librarians make, nor that it is universal. But it is a very easy trap to fall into. A reference client (or "inquirer," but please, not "patron"[3]) is an individual consulting a professional librarian because of a specific need, much as he or she would consult a lawyer or dentist. As a professional consultant, the reference librarian attempts to fill that need. The function of the reference interview, or question negotiation, or whatever one wishes to call the process, is the identification of the client's need. It is in this process that one can easily be misled by the false assumption that the client does not know what he or she is looking for.

I hope to demonstrate that through the interview process the librarian, rather than leading the inquirer to a specific point at which his or her question may be dealt with, may be guided by the inquirer to a similar point, but one more close to the real need of the inquirer. In this process it is obvious that the initial inquiry is likely to be transformed.

It is easier to discuss such a fundamentally abstract, open process as the reference interview if we try to visualize it with a model. There have been a number of attempts to diagram the process; one of the most lucid is that of Robert S. Taylor.[4] Taylor perceives the development and manipulation of a question as metamorphosing through four levels, "visceral," "conscious," "formalized," and "compromised."[5] In proceeding from one level to the next, a question is passed through a number of "filters": "determination of subject," "objective and motivation," "personal characteristics of inquirer," "relationship of inquiry description to file organization," and "anticipated or acceptable answers."[6] To these I would add a sixth filter, personal characteristics of the librarian. As we develop our model, we shall see that the personal style and specific knowledge of the interviewer must play a large part in reaching the fourth stage of question information, the "compromised need," that is, the presentation of the inquiry in a format which enables the interviewer to provide data in a format acceptable to the inquirer.

In discussing the compromised need, we are really dealing with a linguistic phenomenon. Most initial inquiries are perfectly clear to inquirers; they arise from their personal experience. To the reference librarian, they tend to fall into three informal categories: 1. *Misdirected*

Independence. "Where are the encyclopedias?" The librarian must determine whether the encyclopedias, apparently a satisfactory source of information for the inquirer in past experiences, are in the present instance the best first source. If they are, the librarian may wish to determine whether a specific encyclopedia is most suitable. 2. *Vagueness.* "I need to find out about interest rates." Since there is a myriad of sources about interest rates, the librarian must cause the languaged of the inquiry to be narrowed to a stage where some sources may be chosen. 3. *Abstruseness.* "What is the relationship between Buddhist *shomyo* and *matsuri bayashi?"* A very specific question—but unless the librarian is a student of Japanese music, he or she is going to need to find out just what it is the client is talking about.

In each of these instances the inquirer knows what he or she *wants.* What the *need* is may be less certain; it is the province of the librarian to determine that. But in each of the examples above, the need cannot be determined without being filtered through items in the librarian's experience: the librarian's knowledge of the subject, the availability of specific materials, the organization of the material in the library, and the structure of the discipline in question. Thus, to arrive at the mutually useful form of the inquiry, the question must be passed through the librarian's experiential filters as well as guided through the client's.

Hence, our model (see Figure 1). Let us consider the center triangle E as the preliminary goal of the question negotiation process, namely, the mutually acceptable form of the inquiry, or compromised question. On either side, two filters (incorporating Taylor's filters, *supra*): the client's

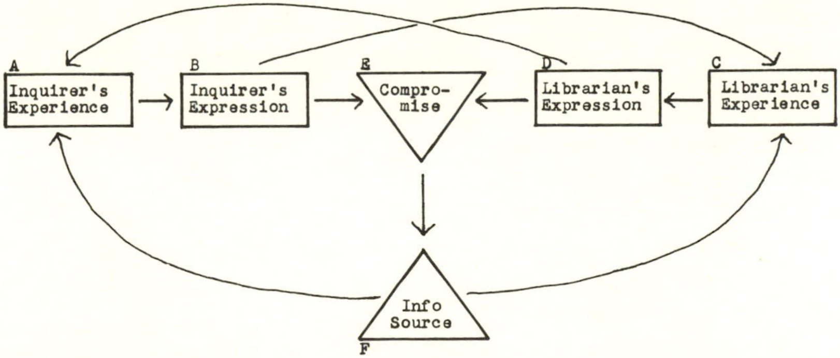

Figure 1

experience and his or her expression of experience, and the librarian's experience and expression. Let us guide a hypothetical inquiry through the model.

A problem arises in the client's experience. Experience is comprised of many elements: training, study, interest, instinct, happenstance, and from all of these, informational need. The need may not yet fully be formed, or more accurately, perceived. But, in any event, the inquirer approaches the librarian and expresses the need (A to B). Thus, the problem is passed through the expression-filter which is, of necessity, a manifestation of language. The problem is perceived by the librarian (B to C) and filtered through his or her own experience, comprised of the same general elements as the inquirer's. Out of his or her experience-filter, the librarian poses certain questions or statements (C to D), expressions of experience again modified by the filter of language. The restated problem, or whatever questions the librarian may pose, now becomes a part of the inquirer's experience (D to A). This cycle may be repeated several times, until a mutually acceptable compromised question is formed (D and/or B to E). From here one or both participants refers to an information source (E to F). Information gained here is assimilated by the experience of the participants (F to A and ideally C). Since the reference interview is an open process, the cycle may continue until the inquirer is satisfied.

In this cycle the informational need factor in the inquirer's experience has been transformed. It similarly has been altered in the experience of the librarian. The concept of a "compromised question" or "negotiation" implies requirements by both participants. The informational need of the librarian must, in fact, be fulfilled before he or she can fulfill that of the client.

The process we have described is necessary because the expression of one's experience usually is not immediately an accurate representation of that experience. Language, and the way we perceive the language of others, is rarely exact. If it were otherwise, librarians would be able to fulfill client's needs (and vice-versa) with far less negotiation than is generally the case. In the course of communication, a major factor in the structuring of one's expression (i.e., the choice of language) is one's own perception of one's experience. A more accurate rendering of both sides of our model might place a third filter, self-perception, between experience and expression (Figure 2).

One's perception of one's own informational need may not be the same as the need itself. It is this self-perception that is changed in one's

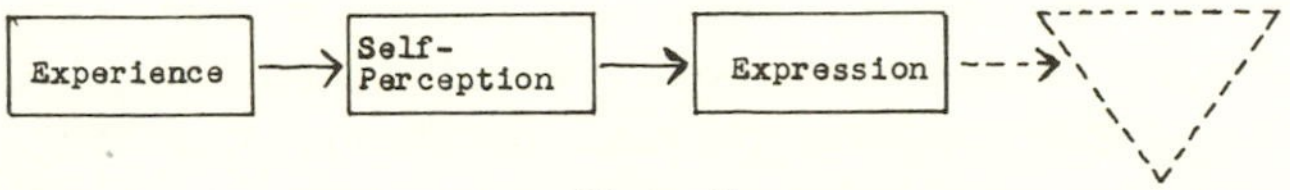

Figure 2

consciousness during the question negotiation process. The need may not fundamentally be altered. In a client's case, the need may not fully be formed in his or her consciousness prior to negotiation. The interview may cause the need to be perceived as being expanded, narrowed, broken up, tied together, reorganized, or a combination of these. Such a transformation should, if the reference librarian is competent, enable the client better to understand the process necessary for his or her arrival at a solution to the perceived problem. From the client's point of view, his or her need as expressed in the compromised question should be perceived as accurate, specific, and comprehensible.

At the same time, these attributes enable the librarian to make choices necessary for a solution of the problem. For a choice of information source, the librarian's perception of the expressed need must be comprehensible within his or her experience, and it must be organized in such a way as to fit a "file structure,"[7] that is, the way that information can best be made available to the client. In our model, then, client and librarian have equally important and interdependent informational requirements, which must be satisfied before an attempt can be made at a solution to the client's problem.

Thus, the ethical dilemma is more insidious than merely assuming that a client does not know what he or she wants. In terms of the goal of a reference interview, a client may not, at the outset, be sufficiently aware of his or her needs to be able to make useful demands of the library. But, as White implies, there is a difference between user needs and user demands.[8] The initial demands are an imperfect expression of imperfectly perceived needs which are defined by the client's experience.

The ethical subtlety lies in the control of the situation, in keeping the interview cycle a balanced process. Rather than one individual imposing his or her experiential framework upon the other's perception, both participants are engaged in altering each other's perception. Yet the process is unlikely to proceed smoothly, if at all, unless one participant pushes it along (one aspect of the "art" of reference service). The cycle is based on the principle of self-disclosure,[9] at its most basic, "You tell me something and I'll tell you something."

This is not merely a statement-response process, though; because an interview is cyclic, a response will provoke its own response. The librarian (or in some instances, the inquirer) must control the course of the interview by responding to questions and posing new questions that will enable both participants to achieve a compromised *demand* that is relevant to the original need.

Where can ethical miscalculations be made? How do reference librarians impose elements of their own experience on their clients', at the expense of honest compromise? The examples which follow probably are not exhaustive, but they are drawn from the author's observations, including of himself. Lest one wonder how librarians can so easily persist in these miscalculations, it should be pointed out that reference clients are generally willing to accept whatever they get, precisely because they are treating librarians as professional consultants. Librarians, like doctors, are perceived by their clients to speak with authority. A client, furthermore, is likely to be sacrificing a certain amount of ego just in admitting that he or she needs help. He or she may not be at ease when asking a stranger for assistance. When the inquirer is not properly aided in perceiving his or her need, he or she may not realize this until after the fact, or may be unwilling to change the course of the interview even knowing that the librarian is not being completely helpful. It is conceivable that one might accept whatever information is provided out of a sense of personal inadequacy, or out of a desire not to hurt the earnest, but misguided, librarian's feelings. In these all-too-frequent cases, the client is likely to go away, apparently happy. He or she is somewhat less likely to come back.

Hence, our catalog of pitfalls. All of these can be perceived as manifestations of the librarian's ego, or suppressions of the client's.

First, we have *imposition of the file structure*, mentioned earlier. In every inquiry, the needed information is locked in one or more prescribed formats, if it is available at all. Taylor perceives part of the negotiation process as "translation," "interpreting and restructuring the inquiry so it fits the files as they are organized [the librarian's] library."[10] These can encompass not only printed resources, but also individuals to whom an inquiry may be redirected.[11] There is always the problem of whether the information is available in a means useful to, or even comprehensible by the client, or for that matter, the librarian. It is also not unusual that the information may not be extractable within the limitations of the client's time. For example, a client may require comparative statistical information apparently available only through lengthy analysis of complex census documents. The participants are faced with the option of redefining the original project to suit existing constraints. But how flexible is the librarian? The file structure itself? More to the point, is the librarian trying too hard to shape the content of the inquiry to fit one particular strategy for a solution, when others are possible? Is it possible to start over and check whether someone has already published a useful analysis of the documents? The author can offer no general solution to this kind of situation, beyond being flexible and encouraging flexibility on the part of the client. Incidentally, the time allotted by the enquirer for a search may be one of the elements in his or her experience most open to negotiation.

Second, there is the matter of *virtuosity.* It is a wonderful feeling when one can, with minimal negotiation, provide a client with exactly what he or she wants. This situation is, however, less common than one would like. It is equally gratifying, more for the librarian than the client, to impress the inquirer with one's ability to provide and interpret data through the use of professional "mysteries"—complex printed sources, computers, or what have you. This can be accomplished fairly often without compromising the clients' needs, although many clients, while growing increasingly confident about the librarian's ability to manipulate the library, may begin to feel left out of the process and therefore may, ironically, mistrust the result.

A third, and particularly problematic trap lies in *goal-orientation.* Most clients appreciate an appearance of efficiency, while librarians, whose attentions are often necessarily divided, can easily be tempted to "wrap things up," perhaps exhibiting their virtuosity at the same time. However, it is better to discourage the idea that once a compromised question has been arrived at, information sources can be supplied which will provide the client with *the answer.* In such a situation, the negotiation cycle has been set up as a closed process. The client has been left to his or her devices with only an opening for a follow-up: "Let's see how you do with this . . . let me know how you make out, OK?" While some situations can adequately be handled this way, many others could better be resolved step by step, treating the negotiation cycle as an open, continuing process. The information provided the client at point F in our model may well raise further questions—it may be the intent of the librarian that it do so. The information may be used only as a step in the clarification of the informational need (F to A). However, the client often needs to be prepared for this. Out of necessity, he or she is oriented toward an informational goal, and may feel that he or she is being put off.

Finally, there is the *Brooklyn Bridge Syndrome*, or the feeling that one must supply the client with something, no matter how inadequate. This is not a problem for which librarians are entirely responsible. The author has been in situations where the library had been turned inside out in pursuit of information that was just not there, while the client, confidence unshaken, insisted that we keep trying. Just for the record, sometimes that last desparate stumble after what was apparently an untamable wild goose has snared the goose. But, to continue a bad metaphor, it is so easy, when one doesn't expect to catch a goose, to offer a turkey. In such instances it might well be ethically more honest to help the client in reconsidering his or her needs, or refer him or her elsewhere.

None of these situations has one simple solution. Effective information service is a matter more of art than science; ethical considerations must be addressed on a case-by-case, person-by-person basis. But it strikes the author that as counsellors, which is what reference librarians are at the most basic level, it is our obligation to keep dialogues open and, simultaneously, relevant to our clients' fundamental requirements. This involves trusting our clients' judgements of their needs, and assuming the most, rather than the least. We possess as much egocentricity and eccentricity as our clients; it is part of being human. The challenge is for librarian and client neither to suppress their own nor the other's experience, but to combine them, share them equally.

NOTES

1. Herb White, "Library Effectiveness—the Elusive Target," *American Libraries*, XI, o. 11 (Dec. 1980),
682-683.
2. *Ibid.*, 682.
3. For a discussion of the difference, see Roger Horn, "Why They Don't Ask Questions," *RQ*, XIII, no. 3 (Spring 1974), 228.
4. Robert S. Taylor, "Question-Negotiation and Information Seeking in Libraries," *College and Research Libraries*, XXIX, no. 3 (May 1968), 178-188.
5. *Ibid.*, 182.
6. *Ibid.*, 183.
7. *Ibid.*, 186-187.
8. White, *op. cit.*, 682.

9. For an excellent essay on this theory, see Mark J. Thompson, Nathan M. Smith and Bonnie L. Woods, "A Proposed Model of Self-Disclosure," *RQ*, XX, no. 2 (Winter 1980), 160-164.

10. Taylor, *op. cit.*, 186.

11. *Ibid.*, 186.

TRIAGE

Joan Meador
Craig Buthod

Webster's Third defines triage as "the sorting and allocation of treatment to patients and especially battle and disaster victims according to a system of priorities designed to maximize the number of survivors," and "the lowest grade of coffee berries consisting of broken material." If thinking of library users as battle casualties is overdramatic, considering them as coffee beans is too mundane. Although the literal dictionary definitions don't quite apply, triage can be a helpful concept of sorting in library reference work. Triage in the public library raises several ethical questions that can be answered only after identifying some of the areas where reference librarians use this technique.

There is triage by amount of time required. This is the easiest and safest form of triage, coming to librarians sometimes by instinct. Place yourself in this scene. It is 12:30 on a busy Saturday afternoon, and your partner is at lunch. Eleven assorted students, do-it-yourselfers, genealogists and trivia addicts face you alone at the reference desk. How do you sort this down to a manageable mob? First you ask, "Who has a quickie?" The three people who just want to find the bathrooms or the elevators are thinned out first off. Next you find that four of the students are looking for magazine articles. A group training session on *The Reader's Guide* takes care of them quickly. A brief tutorial on the library's catalog weeds out two more. Now you're left with the hardcore reference questions. These people who need more of your time and attention have had to wait, but will receive better service now that the crowd has been dispersed.

Next, there is triage by difference in staff knowledge and expertise. The library user with a complicated reference request might best be served by a subject specialist or a staff member with greater skill or experience than by a "new kid." At the same time, use of senior staff to

Joan Meador is Head, Reference Department, Tulsa City-County Library System, 400 Civic Center, Tulsa, OK 74103. Mr. Buthod also is a member of the Reference Department.

answer routine directory-type questions can be a frustrating waste of expertise. Use of junior staff at the reference desk can allow for screening of requests with the routine questions answered directly and the more complicated requests passed on to subject specialists. In order for this method of triage to be successful, reference managers must measure carefully the judgment of the junior staff in deciding what is to be referred. What may be answered to the junior staff's satisfaction may not be answered best or to the user's satisfaction. Self esteem of junior staff is also at risk—users may want to pass them by to get to the "experts." Care must also be taken to avoid the disunity that a "senior staff/junior staff" caste system might cause. In addition to efficiency, another advantage to this sorting lies in the development of the junior staff members who are exposed to all types of reference requests.

The third type of triage, sorting by type of question or user status, presents real ethical dilemmas to reference librarians. The circumstances are familiar to all of us. You have two questions on your clipboard waiting for you to research and report your findings. One is a request for information on side effects of a class of drugs and the other asks what was the top-rated TV show of 1966, a question just broadcast on a radio quiz program. Or a high-level city planner asks for help in researching neighborhood population trends while two giggly sixteen-year-olds want to know about a certain rock and roll singer. Human nature tells us that some questions seem more important than others and deserve more of our time. This form of triage is dangerous. The situation calls on our professionalism to overcome our human nature.

The reference and Adult Services Division of ALA has adopted "A Commitment to Information Services: Developmental Guidelines" in an effort to provide standards of library reference service. This document's section on "Ethics of Service" includes the statement, "Information provided the user in response to an inquiry must be the most accurate possible. Type of question or status of user is not to be considered." It's all well and good that we have in black and white this expression of the RASD Standards Committee's ethic, but practicing reference librarians face all kinds of very real pressure to give preferential treatment to one or another group of users or type of question. There are political pressures such as the call from the mayor's office that seems to demand a drop everything response. Or an influential citizen might get extra attention from the librarian who thinks, "If this fellow doesn't get exactly what he wants, and delivered on a silver platter, I'm sure to hear about it from the boss." The pressure to perform well against standards that measure productivity by the number of questions answered may cause librarians to favor the short and simple. The same effect may result from an overwhelming volume of business.

The tendency to favor some questions or questioners is also influenced by more basic internal pressures and these can be more difficult to deal with than politics. To some there is much more satisfaction in solving a real intellectual challenge in a complicated reference problem than there is in looking in *World Book* again to see if a tomato is a fruit or a vegetable. It just feels good to know that your unique skills enable you to succeed where the next guy in off the street would not. Most of us like to know that the work we are doing is for a good purpose but sometimes it's hard to see it that way when we seem to be doing the entire homework assignment for a teenager over the telephone. It can make anyone uneasy to aid a researcher who is drawing up plans to build a bomb. Then, of course, some of us just don't like genealogists, or bag ladies, or grouchy old men, or people who smell bad.

The effect of all these pressures can be a temptation to provide better service to those users we like or answer those questions that interest us or serve our purposes. In this triage anthing else gets slighted. Responsible librarians must resist this temptation and not just because RASD says to do so. Public librarians are charged with serving all members of the community, not only those with whom they identify. Professionalism dictates that personal preferences be put aside. If we don't avoid moral judgments on what questions are right or deserving of our service, then we will find ourselves trying to impose our own fallible moral standards on the community. Besides being an impossible job, that's not serving our public, that's serving ourselves. If we are to serve the individuals who come to us, we cannot judge the value or importance of their requests.

So, how do we combat the pressures to perform this triage? First we must recognize the real reasons we exist as public librarians. We are in these jobs to serve the individuals who call on us, not just to entertain ourselves with interesting work. The rewards of serving appreciative people or answering interesting questions can be strong motivation, but they are only part of the picture. If we keep in mind that our main purpose is service to our users, and our own intellectual satisfaction is secondary, then personal fulfillment can follow from this well-ordered set of values. Librarianship is a helping profession not just an academic discipline.

Speaking pragmatically, it can be difficult to keep this philosophy in mind and in practice. We need to talk about our service philosophy, think about it, remind ourselves to look for our personal reward in satisfying the faces across the desk or the voices on the phone.

Library administrators can help too. Political pressure to favor one user over another should be relieved by administration support of a policy of even-handed treatment. Knowing in advance that the director will defend your judgment in balancing concurrent demands from "big shots" and "little shots" will make it possible to deal out fair treatment with confidence. Managers should avoid reference measurements that rely only on body counts, since these are so little of the whole picture. Measurement of service should involve more evaluation of the degree of user satisfaction.

The key to successful use of triage is awareness. The pressures to sort out users and their requests will always be with us, and if we pay attention to what we are doing we can use certain forms of triage as positive and useful tools. Awareness comes in knowing that the technique you use is to the benefit of the user, not just the librarian.

REGIONAL PUBLIC LIBRARIES AND REFERENCE ETHICS

Debbie Schluckebier

The adoption of a code of ethics relating to library reference work is vital to the credibility of the reference service in the community. If a reference staff realizes the importance of its work and strives to give correct and unbiased information and assistance to its public, then the library establishes a reputation for accurate and competent work. The reference department of the Daniel Boone Regional Library works to achieve that high level of service while at the same time responding to each individual's question with a personal, friendly manner. Every question we receive over the phone or in person, by child or adult, is answered with our reference or regular collection and with staff knowledge of resources available not only in our collection but in the community as well.

Perhaps the two most basic principles concerning reference work which we emphasize to our staff are (1) protecting the rights of users, and (2) the responsibility of reference workers to keep personal opinion and ideas separate from their work with patrons. These policies are easy to state but are hard to practice. It is difficult to give the same quality of service to a child as to an adult when a reference worker has an expertise in either children's literature or adult reference sources, but not in both. For this reason each reference person in our department has a specialty in which he or she is familiar with the literature in that field. Therefore, if a patron asks a question concerning mutual funds or young adult books on foster homes, for example, we can direct the patron to the reference worker whose specialty is in that area and the patron is given knowledgeable help. This procedure enables the patron to receive the best service we can offer and dispels any feelings of inadequacy on the part of the reference worker.

It is equally difficult to refrain from questioning or influencing a patron's decision about certain topics. Sometimes reference staff find it

The author is Public Services Librarian at the Daniel Boone Regional Library, P.O. Box 1267, Columbia, MO 65205.

hard to give objective assistance to patrons desiring materials concerning topics like abortion, ERA, or busing. One specific example involves a book opposing abortion which is written in a highly dogmatic style with graphic pictures appealing strongly to the emotions rather than the abortion question. All of our reference staff, regardless of their personal feelings on the issue, feel that the book is unnecessarily pictorial in its presentation. Consequently, when a patron asks for materials on anti-abortion, we feel uncomfortable offering this book for selection, even though it may be exactly what the patron desires. We have to remind ourselves that the purpose of our reference department is to serve patron's wants and not to decide for the patron what he needs.

Another important principle reference where ethics become involved is in the dissemination of information. Because of our somewhat unique community, our library has access to more sources of information than an average library might have. In Columbia, Missouri we are fortunate to have several academic and special libraries. The presence of these sources enable us to answer specific questions, and lets the reference department become the middle man in obtaining detailed information for our patrons.

For example, someone may request the symptoms and treatment of an illness. First, we show the individual the general medical information we have in our collection. If the patron desires specific information, we fill out a subject request card which lists a written explanation of the request and the patron's name, address, and phone number. This card is given to the Mid-Missouri Network whose staff will search the University of Missouri and the Veterans Administration Hospital Library collection for specific information. The network then returns the material found and the request card to our reference contact person who notifies the patron of what has been located.

The potential problem of ethics evolves when the patron wants the library staff to interpret the information provided. If the information received is not written in laymen's terms or the meaning is unclear, then the patron might ask for a staff worker's interpretation. In continuing the preceding medical example, the patron may not understand the medical terminology used in the discussion of the illness' symptoms and ask a staff worker what a certain statement means.

The policy that we have adopted is politely stating that we can only provide the information, but not interpret it. We recommend medical dictionaries which can be used by the patron to define the terminology. But we emphasize that we only supply the information, and perhaps the person should consult his physician about the new literature. Medical questions can be especially difficult to handle because an individual's health can be a sensitive subject, and sometimes the patron is anxious about a diagnosis. Consequently, our staff is careful to search for all the pertinent information, but not attempt to analyze it.

Ethics can be also become involved concerning consumer information. Evaluating articles is often subjective, and personal likes and dislikes play an important part in making the right decision about a purchase. We urge patrons to buy products according to the advantages *they* feel are important. However, we have one patron who like to obtain our opinion on consumer matters. She will telephone asking what is the best buy listed in the *Consumer Guide* for a refrigerator, for example. Our usual procedure is to read aloud the condensed article which lists the price and characteristics of specific models. But then she will ask which refrigerator *we* would purchase if *we* were buying one. We then say that it would depend on personal preference, and perhaps the lady should look at the difference models in person in order to make the best decision. If she persists to know our opinion, we offer to send her a copy of the article.

The right of privacy is also an ethical issue that relates to the *Polk City Directory* for Columbia. We often receive long distance calls from credit companies or other concerns wanting to know the place of employment or business phone of a certain individual. If that information is available in the directory, we give it to the caller. But sometimes the person wants more information, such as the names of neighbors. Our reference staff met to discuss whether we felt comfortable releasing the names of "nearbys." We decided it was an invasion of privacy, and it was enough to give only the listing about the person involved. Therefore, we now tell callers that it is against our policy to release names of neighbors. We do not often receive arguments from the callers, and we feel much better about the whole practice for it respects the privacy of the neighbor.

Because we consider our department an important service in our community, we try to uphold the basic code of ethics pertaining to libraries. Hopefully, these examples of our policies confirm that conviction. We are eager to go outside our library's physical boundaries and tap all the possible resources in order to acquire materials or information. But when it comes to offering advice, giving value judgments on materials, or interpreting medical or legal information, we are not as helpful. This type of objective but personal attitude lets us take pride in our reputation for courteous and efficient service.

ACADEMIC LIBRARIES AND REFERENCE ETHICS

Bea Flinner

"Reference service has been defined as the process through which the librarian gives the patron a "body of knowledge." It is also considered that process by which the librarian and the patron find that information together."[1] Unfortunately, both of these definitions seem to imply that patrons are not able to come to the library and carry out searches by themselves. If this is true, how much information should they expect to get from the reference librarian?

A search of the literature has revealed very little on the ethics of "spoon-feeding" students in an academic library. It is sometimes necessary to take action, however. No librarian like to witness a dissatisfied or frustrated patron. When one asks a question, it is obvious that he is seeking an answer, and the reference librarian must make sure that he gets it before he walks out the door. Incidentally, it is important for the librarian to determine the patron's knowledge about the library and the reference tools before deciding on the proper technical level to use with the patron.[2]

Obviously, when research courses are offered, the student will be expected to do library research. But he will not have adequate knowledge of all the tools which are needed to conduct the search process by himself, nor will he know how to go about conducting a search, even though he sat through a special orientation session for his class.

Because reference librarians are expected to be knowledgeable in all subject areas, their skills are frequently used extensively to save the "user any effort in finding his own way through literature and libraries."[3] Peck says that librarians should teach the patron to use the library himself more than he actually does. It is important for college students to learn how to locate information for the purpose of completing class assignments, writing term papers, preparing oral reports and making preparations for graduate school.

Ms. Flinner is Public Services Librarian at the Bethany Nazarene College, Bethany, OK 73008.

When Annette Corth taught a course for reference technicians, she presented to them a set of commandments, with number VI reading "Thou shalt advise thy customer to stay put and keep his or her cool whilst thou seekest the answer to his or her query."[4]

One author suggests that all librarians are viewed by some people "as boys and girls" and the librarians often respond and react to the, "here boy, fetch this," approach by fetching it (if they can)."[5]

Madaus says that "patrons are not to be directed to material—they are to be taken to it."[6]

The question is not how much information and help should be given to students; rather, the question is how much aid should *ethically* be given by the reference librarian, and how much should the student search. For example, a student approaches the reference desk in a mild state of panic, requesting immediate information for a report which is due the next class period. Who wants to see a student suffer from frustration, even though procrastination is not uncommon among the student body? The librarian hurriedly locates sufficient materials, the student expresses his appreciation, quickly copies the information, then makes it to class ten minutes late—but happy! The librarian has done an excellent piece of work from the patron's view—but was it really ethical?

A telephone call is received from a student who requests any six books on a specific subject, which she will pick up in two hours. Is it ethical for the librarian to perhaps take time from other students to locate the needed books while the patron goes about her personal daily schedule? The student does not reveal an compunction, nor any gratefulness, for the service rendered in response to her request. She simply expects the librarian to comply with her request.

Should reference librarians be "ready reference" librarians—e.g., ready to quickly hand over information regardless of whether or not the professor has made an assignment requiring the students to learn how to locate information in the library in a particular discipline?

Constance J. Tiffany and Philip J. Schwarz deal with this prevailing problem in an article on ready-reference. The give excellent solutions via a "KWOC Index to Reference Questions" (Keyword out of context). But what about the ethics of helping the students "slide through" their assignments? Conversely, how can a student find materials when the search process is completely foreign to him?[7]

This all involves the ethics of reference service. Even though an academic library may offer orientation services in the use of the library, there is no possible way to cover all problem points. This simply means that numerous students come to the library, having no idea where to begin a search. Bonus points can be earned on a forthcoming test if a student locates the answer to a specific question. Perhaps the professor says, "But I want the students to locate the information themselves." That is a great idea, but it just doesn't always work that easily.

Another student comes in asking for the same information. Time is so precious for everyone, and it would be ridiculous to go through the same process again or have the student repeat the process, when the answer is known to the reference librarian. Consequently, the information is simply handed to the next student who has "earned" the twenty bonus points without doing a thing.

One assignment was of deep concern to me, and there was a question in my mind as to how I would handle the situation if a second student should ask for the same information. A professor had prepared a list of several topics from which each student was to select one on which he would report. One student came for help, and the material needed was located after a lengthy search. (The student did work along with me, which is highly commendable.) But what if another student had selected the same topic? Would the librarian have run the same gamut again, or would she have played "dumb" and let the student search in vain? Would it have been ethical to hand the citation to the second student, expediting the completion of the assignment?

Often, college students seem to enjoy just looking on while the reference librarian does the searching because the latter has been trained to do reference work and has attained a degree of expertise. She gets paid for her labors, so why shouldn't she do all the work? Where and when does she stop giving out the information (or does she)? Because reference work and the challenge of searching has been a real thrill to me from the day I worked on my first reference question, my personal philosophy is to help students as much as needed, but this does not dispense with the question of the ethics of such a decision.

There are students who are reluctant to use the card catalog. Kelly Patterson has written an article dealing with the "won't lookers," who just are not inclined to make use of this excellent tool.[8] Such an attitude necessitates the reference librarian's searching the card catalog, again involving the ethics of doing the work for the patron.

It is amazing that some college students are shocked to learn that the reference librarian does not have all the answers stored away in her head. She is not a "fact-totem"—an individual who "is too busy stuffing herself with facts to have time to think."[9] On the contrary, she often must search diligently to find those answers that the student thinks is part of her storehouse of knowledge.

There are patrons who take literally the sign above the reference desk which may read "reference-information" or "reference service." In fact, sometimes the reference librarian is now referred to as the "information specialist," which is misleading since "most reference librarians are not experts in information," even though they are knowledgeable about many of the sources.[10]

Samuel Rothstein, a proponent of the "liberal theory" of academic reference service says that information is a crucial concern to many people in all types of libraries and that librarians should give up their reservations about providing answers and information to questions posed by patrons. He believes that it is more important for patrons to have information than to know how to arrive at its source.

In contrast to the liberal theory is the "conservative theory" which says that reference service was an aid to study but that the study itself was to be left to the patron.

A compromise theory between liberal and conservative is the "moderate theory" which combines providing answers to questions posed and attempting to educate the patrons in self-help methods. Is the middle-of-the-road the safest place for the librarian to walk?

A situation involving ethics is that of photocopying. The student may make a copy of the desired material with the intent of recopying it and turning it in to the professor as a completed assignment. This situation places the reference librarian in a difficult situation when it is known that the student intends to take such action. Does the librarian make the professor aware of the fact, or does she just keep quiet? She helped the student.

Some students approach the reference librarian with complete confidence that their needs will be met. "Thank God you're here, you can find anything and I have got to find..." The student appreciates the information and complements the librarian on such wonderful capability of knowing where to look—but what about the ethics of "spoon-feeding" the student? The question remains as to how much information and help the reference librarian should ethically give to the student.

There is no discussion of on-line bibliographic searching in this article, because this excellent service frequently means that none of the work is done by the student until the search is completed—and this opens up another question of ethics which this writer does not care to get involved in at the present. And yet, can one argue against such a practical, efficient and valuable service.

So, the question of ethics in reference service is not resolved. Hopefully, this article will cause other reference librarians in academic libraries to think about the subject, and perhaps come to some conclusions relative to the issue.

BIBLIOGRAPHY

1. Eatough, Judy. "Whither Reference?" *Reference Quarterly* 11:207 (Spring 1972).

2. Howell, Benita J., et al. "Fleeting Encounters—a Role Analysis of Reference Librarian-Patron Interaction." *Reference Quarterly* 16:126-127 (Winter 1976).

3. Peck, Theodore P. "Reference Librarian Recast in a New Role." *Reference Quarterly* 11:212 (Spring 1972).

4. Corth, Annette. "Corth's Commandments." *Special Libraries* 65:473 (October/November 1974).

5. Horn, Roger. "Why They Don't Ask Questions." *Reference Quarterly* 13:226, 228 (Spring 1974).

6. Boyer, Harold N. "Academic Reference Service: Conservative or Liberal Application?" *Southwest Librarian* 24:155-156 (Fall 1979).

7. Tiffany, Constance J. and Philip J. Schwarz. "Need More Ready in Your Reference?—KWOC It!" *Reference Quarterly* 16:39 (Fall 1976).

8. Patterson, Kelly. "Library Think vs. Library User." *Reference Quarterly* 12:366 (Summer, 1973).

9. Isaacson, David. "The Reference Librarian as General Fact-totem." *Wilson Library Bulletin* 495, 495 (April 1980).

10. *Ibid.*

BIBLIOGRAPHIC OVERVIEW: THE ETHICS OF REFERENCE SERVICES

Michael McCoy

In the March 1, 1979 issue of *Library Journal,* a small item appears on page 536:

> Baltimore County, Maryland's North Point Area Branch brought in a medical professional to answer questions about food allergies: if food can make you sick, if it can cause emotional upsets, and if food coloring makes children hyperactive.

This may, of course, be the best way to avoid any problems that arise when answering reference questions about medical, legal, or social problems. But certainly librarians have been asked—and have been answering—such questions all along, and without the advantage of having a professional on-hand. How have librarians approached the problem of library ethics? And what exactly is ethics, as applied to reference service? The answers have not always been clear-cut.

The term reference ethics is an ambiguous one, at best. Felix Ranlett traces the evolution of the term:[1] In 1876, the founding year of ALA, the accepted term was Ideals. This eventually became Etiquette. It was not until 1908 that ALA used the term Ethics. And looking into the card catalog in 1939, Ranlett found: ETHICS, see also SWEARING. But one definition of ethics does not necessarily preclude another. For example, in 1899, Linda Duval of Ohio Wesleyan University stated in an article entitled "The Ethics of the College Library":[2] "to instruct, befriend, control, and inspire these youthful minds is the peculiar duty and privilege of the college librarian." So, the ethics that we see argued about and written about at the turn of the century is not necessarily just a matter of good manners, but rather a philosophy of how any librarian should deal with the responsibility of being the keeper of the books; the one who provides the information to the patron.

Mr. McCoy is a freelance librarian and writer.

Certain ethical problems always seemed to plague the reference librarian. In 1902, Corinne Bacon wrote of her problem with self-censorship:[3]

> I remember carefully explaining to a schoolgirl, who asked for some antiquated books of science, that these books were unreliable and that I could give her some much more up to date, only to find that she was preparing an essay on old scientific text-books, and wanted the very things which I was so eager to prevent her from seeing.

In this case, the confusion could be said to result from that common frustration, not knowing exactly what the patron wants.

However, there were those who believed that the role of the reference librarian should be more than just honoring a request. As Churchill stated in 1903:[4] "And to just such an extent—and it is a very great extent—is the librarian the custodian of public morals and the moulder of public men."

But *is* it the duty of the reference librarian to mold? Mary Wright Plummer dealt with this in her 1916 article, "The Public Library and the Pursuit of Truth":[5]

> Perhaps it is fortunate for truth that the librarian does not know the effects of his books and what is going on in the minds and hearts of their readers, for in every generation fear and distrust of the mental and spiritual processes of others are the dross on the wheels of the chariot that sets out in pursuit of truth.

Never mind about molding public citizens by seeing that only the right information is distributed, she seems to be saying: Keep your nose out of it.

By the end of the second decade of the twentieth century, things were rapidly changing. The World War was soon to envelope us. More people were using the library for more kinds of information. Walter Brown of the Buffalo Public Library addressed some of these problems in his 1917 article:[6]

> A trained technical or vocational teacher would be of considerable value in the library to help with personal counsel and advice . . . and to arrange and supervise reading courses for the workers in various trades, arts, and occupations.

Brown, then, advocated any means to satisfy the patron. The librarian should not be limited to the books on the shelves; in this case, they should bring in a teacher—a human reference tool.

In 1922, an article by Charles Knowles Bolton appeared in "Library Journal."[7] Here, thirty points are listed which outline the ethics of librarianship. Among these: loyalty to the trustees, good health, not criticizing predecessors, and choosing one's friends wisely. Point twenty-five states:

> USE OF HIS NAME: A librarian should stand on neutral ground and should be chary of lending his name to a public controversy to add weight to a contention of local faction . . .

Here, we see the desire for the librarian to be above reproach.

But after the war it became harder not to get involved. The question then became one of how much help should be offered a patron. Frances Bailey tackled this problem in a 1929 article, and her answer is: it depends. Her advice is to leave it up to the individual librarian, who has the best idea of how the staff of each particular library is delegated, the type and amount of material in the library, and the person asking the question. Ethics are not an ideal, to her, which can be summarized in a list, but a subjective problem which must be dealt with case by case.[8]

In a 1930 article by Josephine Rathbone,[9] the suggested code of library ethics is given as they were presented at the ALA mid-winter conference. In section two—Librarian and Constituency—there are two points which would seem to have an effect on the reference service of the library. "The librarian and the staff should . . . take care not to offend against the standards of decorum that prevail in that community or constituency." The section contiunes:

> The librarian, representing the governing body, should see that the library serves impartially all individuals, groups and elements that make up its constituency. In the case of the public library as a non-partisan institution, the books purchased should represent all phases of opinion and interest rather than the personal tastes of librarian or board members. In an official capacity, the librarian and members of the staff should not express personal opinions on controversial questions, as political, religious or economic issues, especially those of a local nature.

So, here are both sides of the issue: the librarian is responsible for the information requested, but the librarian is not responsible for the type of information requested.

In 1931, Katherine Dane explored some of those problems that still plague reference librarians. In the article, she addresses those "legitimate questions sometimes asked of librarians which cannot be answered by them without violating ethical codes."[10] She goes on: "we can refer people to the books in which medical subjects are handled but to attempt to prescribe for patients might land the librarian in the criminal courts." And the ethics she discusses are not always those of the reference librarian. A lawyer who works in a library would be unethical "to give free legal advice when such advice would have to be paid for if given by him in his private capacity."[11] The librarian/lawyer can, however, give out books and refer to certain statements within those books.

In this same article, Dane brings up the question of how much help should be given a student. She cites a phenomenon of the Depression era: crossword-puzzle contests. She asks: "is it ethical to let a reader compete for a prize which would by good rights belong to the librarian. . .?[12] This question would arise again during the 1950's.

In 1936, a cartoon in the ALA Bulletin bears a caption which reads:[13]

> As we draw upon all ages and civilizations for gathering our material so we also serve impartially all the varied peoples who come within our doors: people of many races, many minds, the climbers to the summit, those full of zest of life and the bruised ones, the man eager for quick returns, the scholar and the stranger.

This is a nice, concise definition of the ideals of reference ethics.

In Ratnett's article,[14] he brings up a few more aspects of ethics in library service. For example, impartiality should prevail: circumstances may vary, but each reference question is important to the person asking it. There should be no skimping in one's efforts. He also makes an interesting point: reference librarians should not discuss their work outside the library, adhering to the same ethics as the doctor/patient relationship. He does correlate ethics and manners, and he also feels that the technical and ambiguous jargon that reference librarians tend to use (catalogue, delivery room, newspaper file, etc.) is another area in which the ethics of reference service can stand improvement.

In the same year as Ratnett's article, a column in the *Wilson Library Bulletin* makes this observation:[15]

> Only by yielding type-space, platform-space, and shelf-space to the proponents of all sides of all controversial questions can we give truth the opportunity to prove that time is on its side. The public library is not a commentator of any kind.

Once again, the belief that the reference can only be impartial to all sides by holding no opinion.

In 1944, the ALA's Committee on Intellectual Freedom was asked to reconsider the Library Bill of Rights, after the controversy surrounding Carlson's *Under Cover* in the midst of World War Two. They stated:[16] "Practically, they [the ALA] do *not* accept it when they submit—either willingly or under protest—to pressures of whatever sort which result in denial of freedom of inquiry to the library user." The decorum of the community suddenly seemed to be less important than the right of the librarian to do the job—as a professional—as he saw fit.

After the Second World War, attitudes changed even more dramatically. In January 1946, Ralph Ulveling wrote that the public appears to want "a positive program as distinguished from a laissez-faire program."[17] Ulveling thought that libraries had the "opportunity now to make a statesmanlike contribution to our fellow men,"[18] and encouraged librarians to help eliminate group conflicts through understanding.

Later on that same year, Helen Haines echoed these beliefs when she wrote:[19] "For consider among these new currents [which will have an impact on ethics]:...an awakening social consciousness, transforming old patterns of thought, seeking to replace ignorance and prejudice by knowledge and understanding."

Not all opinions dealing with reference ethics tended to be so lofty. In a 1953 article, Elizabeth Bond discusses some problems that have arisen because of telephone reference service:[20]

> Questions the library should not assume responsibility for answering: "Identification" questions fall into this category with mushrooms heading the list. Identification of anything from a verbal description...is difficult and hazardous, though not so deadly.

She goes on to relate the story of a girl who asked if she could get married by proxy, and the answer was to recommend a lawyer (although it is not clear if a particular lawyer was recommended). She continues:

> If you have a policy about answering—or not answering—certain types of questions, see that the entire staff knows what it is and follows it. But try to have enough flexibility to meet real emergencies effectively and try to see that the staff is trained to recognize these emergencies.

Jack Delaney's 1955 article also deals with the question of ethics. He writes:[21] "I say it's smart to play dumb with certain students, medical patients, and legal clients." He makes the point that the reference librarian's job is to find the books; the patron's to interpret it. He calls anything more, "intellectual bootlegging": over-stepping the bounds of one profession into another.

And in 1955, the problem of the crossword-puzzle contest popped up again, this time with the librarians working the problems and posting the answers. Although this was supposedly to relieve the strain on both the materials and the reference workers, this particular solution met with mixed reactions.[22]

That same year, Dorothy Dengler complained in her article that people were more concerned with finding the "correct" answer rather than thinking for themselves: She submitted:[23]

> In counteracting these trends, the library can perhaps do little, but even that little is important. The librarian can certainly make suggestions to patrons, encourage them to approach their problems creatively, to read books that are uplifting rather than degrading, to read both sides of a question, to continue their process of education in adult discussion groups.

This is quite a responsibility for a reference librarian, particularly in the midst of the McCarthy era.

In the 1960's, there were new ideas of library ethics. In his article, "Ethics: The Creaking Code," John Anderson argues:[24] "Many librarians have been taught that it is against professional ethics to recommend one encyclopedia against another... Do we go to such lengths in other areas of book selection?" Anderson then goes on to say:

> A common admonition to public service librarians is: Never express a personal opinion on controversial issues with a library user. The usual examples are religion and politics. Nowhere in the present Code is it indicated that the librarian should either remain neutral or avoid such discussion.

And in a final assault on the traditional view of reference ethics, William Donovan wrote in a 1969 issue of *RQ*[25] that the reference librarian was always expected to be objective. He, however, advocated a free-association of ideas, "whether it be sex, religion, politics, or Black Power." He goes on: "Librarians, no less than punch press operators, are expected to have opinions..." He sees no reason why these opinions should not be freely shared with the patrons.

So the problem or reference ethics has been, over the years, maybe not a problem of whether or not to help a student, or if a medical question should be answered. The real problem of reference ethics has maybe been in trying to reconcile the ideal with the actual. And while the ideal may remain the same, the actual is only as constant as the individual librarian.

FOOTNOTES

1. Louis Felix Ranlett, "The Librarians Have a Word for It: Ethics," *Library Journal,* 64(17), October 1, 1939, pp. 738-740.
2. Linda M. Duval, "The Ethics of the College Library," *Public Libraries,* 4(9), November, 1899, p.422.
3. Corinne Bacon, "Reference Work from the Librarian's Point of View," *Library Journal,* 27(11), November, 1902, p. 928.
4. Winston Churchill, "The Mission of the Public Library," *Library Journal,* 28(3), March, 1903, p. 116.
5. Mary Wright Plummer, "The Public Library and the Pursuit of Truth," *School and Society,* 4(79), July 1, 1916, p. 17.
6. Walter L. Brown, "The Changing Public," *School and Society,* 6(132), July 7, 1917, p. 5.
7. Charles Knowles Bolton, "The Ethics of Librarianship," *Library Journal,* 47(12), June 15, 1922, pp. 549-50.
8. Frances Bailey, "The Reference Section, Patrons and Personal Assistance," *Wilson Library Bulletin,* 4(1), September, 1929, pp. 11-14.
9. Josephine A. Rathbone, "Suggested Code of Library Ethics," *Library Journal,* 55(4), February 15, 1930, pp. 164-66.
10. Katherine Dana, "What Is Reference Work?", *Wilson Library Bulletin,* 5(7). March 1931, p. 450.
11. Ibid., p. 451.
12. Ibid., p. 452.
13. "Public Library Reference Service," *ALA Bulletin,* 30(6), June 1936, p. 503.
14. Op. cit.
15. S.J.K., "That Library Serves Best...," *Wilson Library Bulletin,* 14(4), December, 1939, p. 314.
16. Leon Carnowsky, "Can the Public Library Defend the Right to Freedom of Inquiry?", *ALA Bulletin,* 38(7), July, 1944, p. 255.
17. Ralph A. Ulveling, "Looking beyond the End of the War," *Illinois Libraries,* 28(1), January, 1946, p. 6.
18. Ibid., p. 5.
19. Helen E. Haines, "Ethics of Librarianship," *Library Journal,* 71(12), June 15, 1946, pp. 849-50.

20. Elizabeth Bond, "Some Problems of Telephone Reference Service," *Wilson Library Bulletin*, 27(8), April, 1953, p. 642.

21. Jack J. Delaney, "Questions to Hedge," *Library Journal*, 80(1), January 1, 1955, p. 48.

22. Martin Erlich, "A Puzzling Problem," *Wilson Library Bulletin*, 30(4), December, 1955, pp. 326-29, 332.

23. Dorothy June Dengler, "Conformity and the Public Library," *Wilson Library Bulletin*, 30(5), January 1956, p. 387.

24. John F. Anderson, "Ethics: The Creaking Code," *Library Journal*, 91(19), November 1, 1966, p. 5335.

25. William Donovan, "The Reference Librarian and the Whole Truth," *RQ*, 8(3), Spring 1969, pp. 196-99.

THE REVIEWING OF REFERENCE BOOKS

A. J. Walford

Reference books, because of their frequent dictionary/directory form or encyclopaedic nature, are difficult subjects for well-tempered, responsible reviewing. One does not normally read through them in order to make judgments. The reviewer, pressed for time, may go no further than glance at the introduction and take sample dips into the text, resisting the temptation to parade his/her own command of the subject. Apart from stating, clearly and succinctly, the aim, scope and contents of a reference work, the author's qualifications and the presence/absence of bibliographies, indexes and cross-references, the conscientious reviewer must evaluate, and evaluate comparatively. The book has to be related to what has already been published on the subject.

According to Dr. Sarton, no book deserves unconditional praise.[1] But the praise or blame must be precisely qualified. The following actual unsigned review is an example of woefully imprecise, perfunctory reviewing, no less apt for being some fifteen years old:

> *A Concise Encyclopedia of Metallurgy,* by A.D. Merriman, 1965. 1178 pages . . . Any book dealing with the interpretation of metallurgical terms would certainly be welcome. Many new terms have been coined in recent years, and I am sure that this volume in greater or less measure will help fill the void.
>
> In this concise encyclopedia of metallurgy, the author attempted to present a more direct meaning of some of the terms, included new terms, and yet kept the book as compact as possible. The book has been printed in a size easy to handle and store.
>
> I reviewed some of the older metallurgical dictionaries in order to make a comparison. There are many terms that have been deleted and there are some terms to which additional material has been added. Some of the terms and definitions are controversial, but overall this book will greatly help the student, the engineer,

---

Mr. Walford is the author of *Guide to Reference Materials,* and writes extensively on reference works.

and scientist keep abreast of the advances in metallurgical terms.

In the table of contents, I feel that the book would be easier to use if the author had included a listing of the illustrations and tables with figure, table and page number.[2]

This review makes no mention of Merriman's earlier work, *A Dictionary of Metallurgy* (1958), on which the *Concise Encyclopedia* is largely based. In fact, owners of the earlier dictionary had no need to look further. The *Concise Encyclopedia* contains 249 diagrams and 235 tables, but this is not stated in the review, nor are actual examples of short/lengthier entries given. Finally, comparison with other metallurgical dictionaries is only hinted at, whereas in fact Merriman's definitions are fuller and more numerous than those in, for instance, Bates' *Metallurgical Dictionary* (1953).

By contrast, the following review, also unsigned and of similar length, is concise, informative, evaluative and comparative, as well as compulsive reading:

A Traveller's Guide to Health. James M. Adams, B.Sc., M.B., lieut.-colonel, Royal Army Medical Corps. London, Hodder & Stoughton (for the Royal Geographical Society). 1966. pp. 189 . . . This admirable and low-priced little book exactly fits its function, replacing the medical chapters of the Royal Geographical Society's *Hints to Travellers,* long out of date. It is primarily designed for the small scientific expedition, without a doctor, which will be visiting remote areas in increasing numbers as the International Biological Programme gets into its stride in 1967. But the explorer, the mountaineer, and even the tourist will find much of value in it. It covers preparatory planning (including training and immunisation), general principles, diseases peculiar to the tropics, and medical problems in cold regions. Appendices contain suggestions for further reading and a list of dental equipment for use in trained hands. While this volume is very difficult to fault, it is a pity to see "natural resistance", in the sense of physical fitness, lingering on in the section on infectious diseases, and there is no reference to smallpox modified by vaccination--that bugbear of diagnosis. The advice on the prevention of the diarrhoeal diseases from infected food might have been summarised as "peel it, cook it, forget it."[3]

Both the above examples were unsigned, a practice that is now becoming less frequent. Even the *T.L.S.* switched to signed reviews in 1974. At the other extreme, the journal *Contemporary Psychology* prefaces reviews with qualification data on the reviewer as well as on the writer of the book reviewed.

To review a new edition of the *Encyclopaedia Britannica* must always be a major assignment. C. K. Ogden, a Cambridge don, produced a masterly appraisal of the 1926 edition of the *Britannica* in the *Saturday Review of Literature* that has remained a classic of its kind. It was a sustained and devastating exposure of omissions and lack of scholarship, although Ogden disclaims prejudicial treatment. He stipulated that 'a just criticism makes much use of good points and only mentions flaws for the purpose of future improvement'. However, he concludes that the 1926 *Britannica* is a more worthy record of our time than anything that has hitherto been published'. The reader of the review is left dazzled and also somewhat bemused.

There are set points, then, that ought to be borne in mind when reviewing or appraising reference books. The 'marking schedule' used by committee members for assessing books submitted for the Library Association's McColvin and Besterman medals is relevant here. These two medals are awarded annually for an outstanding reference work and bibliography respectively, published in the year concerned, and marks (out of ten in each case, if preferred) are allotted under the following ten heads:

1. The authority of the work and the quality and kind of the articles or entries.
2. The accessibility and arrangement of the information.
3. The scope and coverage.
4. The style.
5. The relevance and quality of the illustrations.
6. The quality of the indexing.
7. The adequacy of the bibliographies and references.
8. The up-to-dateness of the information.
9. The physical presentation.
10. The originality of the work.

Not all the foregoing points are automatically applicable. I offer the following outline of a review which covers most of the criteria:

Keegan, John, ed. *World Armies*. London, Macmillan, 1979. xii, 843 p. £22.50.

Editor: Senior Lecturer on War Studies, Royal Military Academy, Sandhurst.

Contributors: 16 in all (10 from the R.M.A., Sandhurst).

Aim: To set each army of the 150 countries covered 'in its domestic context, historical, social and political as well as military.'

Contents: Countries A-Z. Headings under each: History and introduction - Strength and budget - Command and constitutional status - Role commitment, deployment and recent operations - Organizations - Retirement, training and reserves - Equipment and arms industry - Rank, dress and distinctions - Current developments. Statistics up to 1977.

Balance: The Argentine army is allotted 7½ pages, nearly as much space as for the British army (9½ p.), although it has fought no war for a century. Reason? - because of the conspicuous political role it plays in national affairs.

Appendices: 2 (*eg,* 1: Africa: armies of nations formerly British or French colonies: an historical note). Additional data on 10 countries.

Format, etc.: A handsome quarto, 10½" x 8½". Well laid out.

Deficiencies: No index (although a detailed contents list); no bibliographies (although a few footnote references). No illustrations or maps.

Comparison: *World Armies* adds flesh to the bare bones provided in *The Military Balance* (international Institute of Strategic Studies, London), from which Keegan has had permission to draw freely. *The Military Balance* has the advantage of being annual and cheap (£4). (*World Armies* is however, to appear regularly.) The slightly older *Defense and Foreign Affairs Handbook, 1978* (London & New York, Copley & Associates, S.A. 1978. xvi, 757p. $50) has political, economic and defence data on 190 countries: short bibliography; who's who; tables and maps). *World Armies* compares favourably, despite its price, with the statistical-directory type of information in the U.S.-slanted *Reference Handbook of the Armed Forces of the World* (4th ed. New York & London, Praeger, 278p.

$20) and *The Almanac of World Military Power* (4th ed. San Rafael, Calif., Presidio Press, 1980, xi, 418p. $40), which has numerous black-and-white maps (cluttered with detail) plus background information more regularly available in *Statesman's Year Book* or *Europa Year Book.*

Readership: For the university, college and larger public reference library, as well as libraries specializing in the field. Undergraduate and graduate level.

So much for the review. But what of the reviewer? Ken Kister, a full-time American reference-book critic, has outlined the qualities considered necessary for the good reference-book reviewer thus:

1. Ability to write clearly, succinctly and sometimes quickly.
2. A thorough and comparative knowledge of reference materials and their make-up, characteristics and uses.
3. An objective stance.
4. An honest and independent spirit.[5]

Dr. Sarton has written a final word of comfort for the conscientious book-critic: "When a reviewer has written a faithful review of a book, he has rendered a great service to the author and publisher".[1] Bruce D. Macphail, echoing this sentiment, sees book reviews as an adjunct to the editorial process, as well as an effective method of promotion. "Perceptive reviewers often go beyond analysis of the work to compare it with other works and, more important, to suggest directions in which further study should proceed."[6]

REFERENCES

1. Sarton, G. 'Notes on the reviewing of learned books', *Science,* v.131, no.3408, 22 April 1960, p.82-87.
2. *Journal of the Institute of Metals,* v.32, no.11, July 1965, col.944.
3. *The Lancet,* no.7464, 17 September 1966, p.624.
4. *Saturday Review of Literature,* 23 October 1926.
5. Kister, Ken. 'Wanted: more professionalism in reference book reviewing', *RQ,* v.19, no.2, Winter 1979, p.144-8. Also in his contribution, 'Reference book critic', in *What else you can do with a library degree,* edited by Betty-Carol Sellen (Syracuse, N.Y. Gaylord, 1980), p.175-81.
6. Macphail, Bruce D. 'Book reviews and the scholarly publisher', *Scholarly Publishing,* v.12, no.1, October 1980, p.55-63.

FORTHCOMING IN THE REFERENCE LIBRARIAN

REFERENCE SERVICES FOR CHILDREN & YOUNG ADULTS

Definitions, Services and Issues. . . . . Shirley A. Fitzgibbons
Young Adult Reference Services in the Public Library. . . . .Mary K. Chelton
From the Front Lines: Practical Reference Work With Children and Young People. . . . . Gretchen Wronka
Helping Young People Connect With Their World. . . . . Emma Cohn
Public and School Library Cooperation: Applications for Reference Librarians. . . . . Barbara Will Razzano
Special Patrons, Special Needs: Reference Services for Young Adults. . . . . Audrey B. Eaglen
The In House Production of Informational Products for Adolescents and Children: Problems and Prospects for Reference Staffs. . . . . Bernie Luckenbill
Vertical Files: Versatile Library Tools, So Why Aren't You Using Them. . . Catherine S. Chang
Reference Services for Young People and Children: A Viewpoint. . . . . Pat Payne
Doing the Missing Book Boogie. . . . . Carole M. Hastings
Eggs to Omelets Without Eggshells. . . . . David P. Snider
Please Interrupt Me. . . . . Diana Young
Children's Questions: Reference Interviews With the Young. . . . . Linda Ward Callaghan
Information Needs of Young Users. . . . . Judith Rovenger
Sources of Information: Reference Work With Children. . . . . Barbara Rollock
Meeting the Information Needs of the Child of Elementary School Age. . . Gertrude B. Herman

Stalking the Elusive Regional Material. . . . . Anitra T. Steele
Reference Needs of Children and Young Adults in Public Libraries. . . . . Evie Wilson
From Diamonds to London: Reference Research By Children. . . . . Hazel Rochman
Selecting Reference Materials for Library Service to Children and Young Adults. . . . . Mary Alice Deveny

VIDEO TO ONLINE: REFERENCE SERVICES & THE NEW TECHNOLOGY

Micrographics and Reference Services. . . . . William Saffady
Vid-Tele-Reference: The New Frontier. . . . . Helen M. Gothberg
Taking it to the Streets: Videotext and the Reference Librarian. . . . . Mark W. Bendig
Interlibrary Loan and the New Technology. . . . . Noelene Martin and M. Sandra Wood
Online Circulation Systems and Reference Services. . . . . Trish Ridgeway and Larry Mitlin
Computers, Reference and Revolution. . . . . Robert Hauptman
Are Computers Necessary. . . . . Norman Stevens
Why You Should Use Both Free Text Terms and Controlled Vocabulary in Online Searching. . . . . Sally Knapp
Online and Manual Searches, A Comparison. . . . . Bruce A. Shuman
Online Reference...No Longer an Option. . . . . Betty Unruth
Choosing the Appropriate Online Database. . . . . Michael Halperin
Online Reference and Fee-Based Online Services: A Plan for Peaceful Coexistence. . . . . Carolyn G. Weaver
Techniques for Effective Online Literature Searching. . . . . Mary L. McMartin
Computer Literature Searching: The First Year in a Small Liberal Arts College. . . . . Douglas W. Cooper
Database Subject Searching Comes to a College Library. . . . . Ruth E. Turner
Online Reference Services in a University Library. . . . . Russ Chenoweth
Microcomputers and Reference Service. . . . . Robert Burgess
Adapting Online Database Systems for Reference Service. . . . . Alison Cuyler

The Librarian-Information Specialist and the Client: Reference Interview Revisited. . . . . Jitka Hurych

Locating Reference Sources; So-Long Printed Indexes, Hello Terminal. . . Barbara A. Moore and Ronald Fingerson

The Impact of Online on Organization of Reference Services. . . . .Cerise Oberman